THE
QUEEN ALEXANDRA
HOSPITAL HOME

for disabled ex-servicemen
Gifford House
Worthing

A HISTORY

Gladys, Marchioness of Ripon in whose memory Gifford House was founded

THE
QUEEN ALEXANDRA HOSPITAL HOME

for disabled ex-servicemen
Gifford House
Worthing

A HISTORY

David S. Farrant

Phillimore

1997

Published by
PHILLIMORE & CO. LTD.
Shopwyke Manor Barn, Chichester, West Sussex

ISBN 1 86077 055 X

Printed and bound in Great Britain by
BOOKCRAFT LTD.
Midsomer Norton

CONTENTS

◆

This book is dedicated to the patients and staff of the Queen Alexandra Hospital Home since its founding in 1919. This is their story of vision, courage and cheerfulness. I hope that it is worthy of their memory.

It is also dedicated to my mother who inculcated in me a love both of words and of history.

LIST OF ILLUSTRATIONS

◆

ACKNOWLEDGEMENTS

◆

My thanks first and foremost to Miss J.M. Holgate, MVO, who first suggested that this book should be written and then gave me every support possible, not least in providing me with access to papers, journals, press cuttings, minutes, photographs and other information held in the archives of Gifford House together with her own reminiscences covering 46 years. I hope that this account will be an adequate response and a recognition of the part she has played in its history.

Many people who have been associated with Gifford House in various capacities over the years have given me ideas, information and their stories, which have helped me to paint a balanced picture and a human one. I would like to thank especially Sidney Bristow, Frank Burge, May Cheesman, Mollie Cormick, Tommy Doyle, John Ferries, Leslie Gunn, Barry Houghton, William Lunn, Daphne Morris, Shirley Sullivan and Sir Philip Ward.

Most of the material for this book is held in Gifford House but for my researches elsewhere I am indebted to Roy Rates, and to Sarah Paterson and Roderick Suddaby of the Department of Printed Books and the Department of Documents respectively at the Imperial War Museum.

Carol Tyler has led me through the vagaries of floppy—and other—disks with a remarkable tolerance and good humour.

This project finally got up steam when Noel Osborne, Managing Director of Phillimore & Co. Ltd. gave me every encouragement to go ahead, and Nicola Willmot has been an ever-smiling and patient guide throughout the production process.

But without the impeccable filing and storage of so much material dating back to the First World War and the following decades, there would have been merely the bare bones of a story and I owe a great debt to those often unnamed people whose work is reflected in almost every page of this volume.

Queen Elizabeth The Queen Mother during her visit to Gifford House in 1989 with Maj-Gen. Sir Philip Ward, Chairman

CLARENCE HOUSE
S.W. 1

My first visit to the Queen Alexandra Hospital Home was in 1928, in Roehampton. Six years later I was able to see the Home in its new surroundings in Worthing. I became President in 1953 in succession to Queen Mary. Thus my association with the home goes back a long way.

This book is the record of a very special place, originally conceived for the benefit of men wounded and disabled in the First World War. At that time there was nowhere for such men to live out their lives in anything other than bleak and impersonal institutions.

The history of the Queen Alexandra Hospital Home is a tribute to the vision of one woman — Gladys, Marchioness of Ripon. During times of much social change, a devastating Second World War and to the present day its catalogue of care and concern is unmatched. Through those years I have seen the progress made in new developments and facilities and in enhancing patient care. Always I have been impressed by the characteristic cheerfulness and high morale of the patients and the staff.

May the home continue to flourish and may it uphold the fine traditions which it is so worthily maintaining.

Elizabeth R

The Changing Value of the Pound

The purchasing power of the pound has fluctuated during the 80 years covered in this history. The comparable purchasing power of £1 in 1995 is shown below:

	£
1915	42.60
1920	21.30
1925	29.82
1930	33.13
1935	37.28
1938	33.89
1950	16.57
1955	13.31
1960	11.83
1965	10.07
1970	8.06

(Source: *Whitaker's Almanac*, 1997, p.599)

CHAPTER 1

◆

THE KING GEORGE HOSPITAL

Historians, politicians and sociologists will forever analyse and comment upon this country's pre-paredness or, as some would say, lack of it, for the demands of the First World War. Whatever the debate about armaments and strategic planning aided by the wonderful gift of hindsight, this history looks at one very special aspect of that war—the continuing provision of medical facilities for the wounded and disabled. It is a history which shows how the response was made to an unprecedented demand for nursing care. It is a history of innovation in tackling new problems and of refusing to be daunted by apparently intractable situations and insurmountable numbers. However, its main theme is the visionary thinking of specific people and the way in which they set out to turn into reality ideas which at the time must have seemed impossibly challenging. These innovators har-nessed the efforts of their friends and of their many contacts. Most of their work was done on a completely voluntary basis (a not uncommon feature of British society) and it was done with dedication. Their work set new standards of care for the disabled and many of their ideas are now part of the basic assumptions which today form the planning basis of a wide range of nursing institutions, both civil and military.

The beginning of this remarkable saga is in London, on a site bordered by Stamford Street, Cornwall Road, Waterloo Road and Doon Street, close to Waterloo Station. In 1915 this was the location of an unlovely, unoccupied building which was planned to become His Majesty's Station-ery Office. This solid edifice must have looked incongruous, surrounded as it was by tiny private houses in this residential area of south-east London. These houses had become soot-stained over the previous century and presented a monotonous aspect. The surrounding streets were narrow—Doon Street would more properly be designated an alley. A little row of shops faced this build-ing—a barber, a wheelwright, a furnishing undertaker and a shop selling milk and eggs. Also in the shadow of the building was a toy and doll repairer. It was possible to glimpse the Thames and wharves where barges loaded and unloaded in the typically cosmopolitan atmosphere of the dockside. On the side of the building nearest to the station, the view was of a large graveyard which perhaps gave at least some relief from the vista of the housetops.

The building, with its rows of immense windows set in iron frames, was far from completion, and it was realised that a hospital could emerge from the internal chaos common to construction sites, if there were a will to change its designated purpose. The War Office saw an opportunity to begin to meet the overwhelming demand for beds which was becoming more pressing as month succeeded month during this war which had failed to meet so many expectations for a speedy resolution. As the Army Medical Corps personnel stumbled about in the chaos of this unfinished building, they could indeed see that this might well provide a haven for sick and wounded soldiers.

At this point, the role played by the British Red Cross Society and the Order of St John of Jerusalem became crucial. Both societies were playing a significant part in providing medical care and support both at home and in the fields of conflict. They were aware of the multitudinous demands being made on the highly efficient Army Medical Department in many parts of Europe and they expressed the wish that this proposed hospital should be a Red Cross hospital. The two

1

1   *The King George Hospital*

societies (henceforward known as the Joint Societies) could not undertake to assume all the financial responsibilities incurred in the construction process but, if the War Office would carry out the costly and elaborate structural alterations, the societies would equip the wards, the operating theatres, the dispensaries, the special departments, the chapels, the day rooms for the patients and the quarters for the staff. For the duration of the war, they also guaranteed to contribute up to £500 per week (£20,000 at today's prices) towards the wages of the staff and personnel, under military administration. The Army Council, on their part, undertook to carry out all the necessary structural alterations and to transform this shell of a building into a hospital. So we see for the first time in this history the invaluable and fundamental part played by voluntary aid. It was an aid which was to perform with distinction alongside the Army Medical Service and which was to prove to be indispensable in its support activities.

So what did this building offer? Its length was approximately 400 feet, its width 100 feet. There was a ground floor with a basement hall and five stories above, completed by a flat roof with the cupolas of lifts and a series of water tanks. The type of heating was still fairly innovatory, for the comment made at the time was that the building 'is warmed by what is known as "Central Heating"'.

The special qualifications which suited it for a hospital were many. Being built of concrete and iron, it was fireproof. It had never been occupied. The upper floors had excellent lighting and ventilation, for the external walls were practically all windows. At ground level a platform like a quay ran the whole length of the building; whilst it had been designed to handle stationery and papers, it was ideal for the unloading of ambulances, being in a quiet street and under cover. From that platform, ten lifts, each capable of taking stretcher cases, ascended to each of the eventual wards. Even the flat roof, one and a half acres in size, was ideally suited for leisure purposes and was to be regarded as the 'grounds' of the institution.

The alterations to be made were considerable. They were carried out under the direction of the Director of Barrack Construction, Mr. H. B. Measures. One can imagine that the building contractors may well have questioned the decision to change the use of the building and to wonder about the competency of the planners. Such is the common lot of any architect or contractor, and many are reconciled to the adage that 'the customer is always right' however late the stage in a building project. But the revision of the plans seems to have gone ahead smoothly with the exception of a strike by the plumbers, apparently related to the difficulties with the sanitary arrangements.

The basement was devoted almost entirely to stores. It also housed the chapel and a concert hall capable of holding some 700 patients. Quietly located at the far end of the floor was the little mortuary chapel. The five floors above were divided into wards of differing sizes, together with ward kitchens, linen rooms, medical officers' rooms and day rooms for the patients. There were six operating theatres with accompanying anaesthetising and sterilising facilities. The kitchens, capable of cooking for over 2,000, were on the fifth floor. The magnitude of the operation is underlined by some figures taken from official data. The partitions, creating 63 wards, required 46,500 square feet of partly opaque glass and asbestos sheeting weighing over 300 tons (not an aspect which would have been favoured by modern planners!). The length of the corridors represented a walk of over two miles. The floor covering called for an order of nine acres of linoleum.

The resident population was in the region of 2,000, with accommodation for 1,650 patients, 17 resident medical officers and a staff of close on 300 nurses, as well as orderlies. The specification and ordering of the scientific and professional equipment was under the direction of Sir Frederick Treves, Bart., Sergeant Surgeon to H.M. The King. He was supported by the Comptroller of H.M. Stationery Office and by the Comptroller of Supplies in H.M. Office of Works. This exercise was carried out with due regard to the fact that every penny of the donors' money had to be spent to the best advantage; doubtless the purchasing power of the government departments involved ensured that good value for money was achieved.

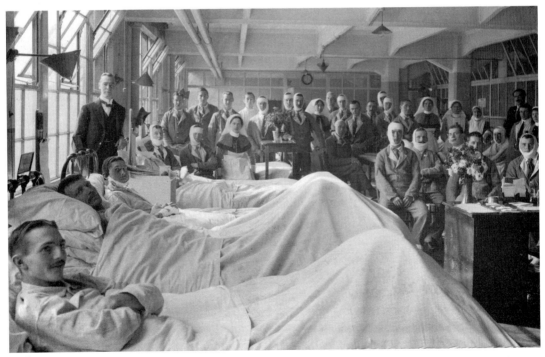

2 *One of the wards*

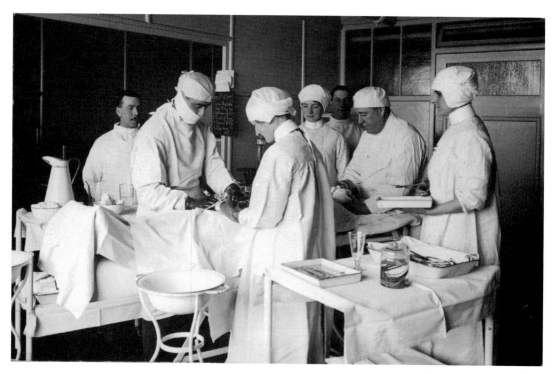

3 *An operating theatre. The black board on the wall gives the date as 11 October, the first operation of six beginning at 2pm under an Army Captain. The patient's eyes are open!*

The equipment of a hospital is generally estimated at so much per bed. The sum of £25 (£1,025 at today's prices) was decided upon. This figure included the general equipment and furnishing not only of the ward, but of all its dependencies, the providing of drugs and medical appliances, the purchasing of the vast amount of linen required and the supplying of the seemingly endless list of requirements of a hospital. So the commitments made by the Joint Societies were heavy. As standard equipment, every one of the 1,650 beds (if placed end to end they would have covered nearly three miles) was provided with a folding chair, a locker and a standard lamp. The supply of the necessary crockery, hardware and glass was a further charge to be contained within the £25 target sum. One special charge which was excluded from the above calculations was the costly equipment required for the six operating theatres. The British Farmers' Red Cross Fund allotted over £4,000 (£160,000) which enabled these to be fully set up and also the provision of the costly X-Ray installation. (It would be tedious always to show the present day purchasing value of the £; readers are referred to the Table at the beginning of this book which shows those details and which indicates the extent of the financial commitments, both expenditure and revenue.) For those patients who were not confined to bed, Day Rooms were provided which could be regarded as a club room or a casino depending upon individual preference. Sir Frederick Treves describes these rooms in somewhat dramatic language:

4 *Day room*

Here at last (the patient) is free of the ward, with its sickly sights, its suspicious smells, its horrid sounds. Here he is free from the gentle tyranny of the nurse. He can once more express himself in such language as he finds the freest and easiest, since in the wards unrestrained speech is limited to whispers between near bed companions. He can smoke, can write letters, can look over the illustrated papers, play a game of cards, and even be beguiled by the hoarse music of the gramophone.

Six such rooms were provided, each accommodating up to 70 men. They were designed by Lady Wernher, who also paid for the cost of two of the rooms.

The roof of the building represented the only 'grounds' available to the hospital. It commanded a fascinating view over the Thames from Westminster to the Tower and to the uplands of Kent, and on a clear day the Surrey hills could be seen. Here was a place to sit in the sun, away from the jostling life of the wards and to enjoy the solitude which many needed. On the roof there were 25 revolving shelters which could be turned so as to avoid the rain and wind or to catch the sun. Without these, the roof would have been a desert and a valuable therapeutic element would have been lost.

The chapel, below the ground floor, was furnished by Adeline, Duchess of Bedford. It had accommodation for a congregation of 250, an organ and a vestry. The Duchess supervised personally the furniture for the chancel and the altar. On the fifth floor was the Chaplain's Quiet Room, where Communion could be celebrated for those unable to attend chapel and where quiet consultation and pastoral care could be exercised in confidence.

An appeal was made for donations to finance the setting up of the hospital on the basis of the standards described above. The response was very prompt and very generous. Within a few weeks every one of the 1,650 beds had been given. Doubtless the wish to give the best attention to soldiers wounded in the war was a strong motivator as well as a recognition by the civilian population of the role which the Army was playing in the defence of the nation and freedom.

5   *A view from the roof towards St Paul's Cathedral*

The response came from every part of the community. Among the donors of beds were their Majesties the King and Queen, Queen Alexandra, the King and Queen of Portugal and Queen Amelie of Portugal. Cora, Countess of Strafford, presented 22 beds given by a number of Americans. The theatrical profession also gave 22, the Civil Service 14, the 3rd Army Corps 18 beds. The Southdown Laundry gave two beds plus £3 per week towards the cost of maintenance. Other donors included a bench of magistrates, a body of special constables, the Blackmore Vale Hunt, the London Society for Women's Suffrage, and the Irish Lady Golfers. Groups of schoolchildren sent in their collections of pennies; one asked for a photograph of their bed 'with a soldier in it'. Many beds were donated in memory of loved ones, some of whom had been killed in service e.g. 'soldiers of the 1st Battalion Cheshire Regiment who, leaving Londonderry on 15 August 1914, fell at Mons'. Donations came from India, Burma, Ceylon, New Zealand and Australia. Fiji gave two roof shelters. Over one bed was placed the tablet, 'In Memory of Dad'.

King George V showed a personal interest in the progress of the hospital which he was graciously pleased to name. When he inspected the hospital, although only two floors were open, he declared to the Chairman of the Joint Societies Committee, Sir William Goschen, his delight with the magnificent work that had been done.

The Queen sent the linen and blankets for the two beds which she had given, embroidered with her cypher. Queen Alexandra gave the cross set with moonstones, and the vases for the mortuary chapel. On the pendiment of the cross, which, with the front of the altar, can still be seen in the Gifford House chapel today, is the inscription:

> Jesus calls,
> Now comes Peace.
> From Alexandra.

The hospital was opened for the admission of patients on 26 May 1915. The number of those seeking admission met the expected volumes and the beds were soon fully occupied; on one day, the number of admissions was, in fact, 1,652, the full complement of beds. The numbers recorded by the Company Office, where all the administration was handled, show the extent of the treatments given. For example, during the 12 months from 5 October 1915 to 30 September 1916, over 23,000 patients passed through the hospital:

Received from Queen Mary's Hospital, for discharge	2,188
Ordinary discharges, fit for duty	4,795
Discharged for light duty only	3,567
Discharged the service after convalescence	2,649
Transfers to units or convalescent hospitals	2,856
To auxiliary hospitals	4,084
Furlough to men from the Expeditionary Forces	3,517

Patients were received from all parts of the world—France, Gallipoli, Persian Gulf, East and West Africa, Egypt, Salonika, and India, as well as transfers within the United Kingdom.

The work of individual departments is graphically demonstrated by the volumes handled and the types of cases. The X-Ray Department made over 6,500 examinations in the time quoted above. They received from overseas a very large proportion of soldiers with serious injuries to the head, spine and jaw and these sometimes gave particular difficulty when trying to localise the injuries. The Bacterial and Pathological Departments made over 400 separate examinations and reports, having many overseas cases which called for research, e.g. dysentery. The Dental Department dealt with nearly 300 cases requiring highly specialised treatment for gunshot wounds of the jaw and face. An addition to the hospital was the department for Massage and Electro-Therapy

6   *The Dispensary*

with a full plant of gymnastic apparatus. The many cases of shell-shock and of limb deformity meant that they carried out over 86,000 treatments.

There were auxiliary hospitals closely linked with the King George Hospital. These were two Red Cross (Benfleet Hall, Sutton, and Kingston, Surbiton and District) and two under the aegis of the Order of St John of Jerusalem (Gifford House, Roehampton and Percy Schools, Isleworth). These had a total of 860 beds. In addition, Queen Mary's Hospital at Roehampton had the task of fitting artificial limbs and other appliances. To link each of these locations, the Transport Department was established with a fleet of six ambulances which were garaged at the hospital. In the first 15 months of its operating, 22,372 patients were carried and 116,808 miles travelled. This work was also under the supervision of the Joint Societies. Another duty of this department was Air Raid Duty. On receiving a call that a raid was expected (the target was 30 minutes' notice) three ambulances were to report at the rendezvous for the South Eastern District, equipped with blankets, pillows, stretchers and First Aid outfits, and with two orderlies in attendance.

As war casualties continued to flow in to the King George Hospital, it was becoming increasingly clear that they could not all be satisfactorily treated for their immediate and longer term needs. The number of beds at the hospital seems generous by modern day standards when the 'peace dividend' is showing itself in radical adjustments to military planning and armed forces provision. However, as the war progressed and the number of casualties mounted, the hospital found itself in dire need of additional facilities for the wounded.

Lady Ripon, whom we shall meet in the next chapter, was in the forefront of the campaign to increase the number of beds. This involved her in searches in other parts of the country, one such area being Staffordshire. In the summer of 1916 she wrote to the Mayor of Stafford asking for his support in identifying accommodation at the North Staffordshire Infirmary; letters of support were also sent from the Duchess of Sutherland and Lord Dartmouth.

It is interesting to speculate on the impact of this correspondence from a group of such influential people, and one imagines that there must have been a long and heart-searching discussion amongst the members of the Infirmary House Committee (to whom the Mayor had forwarded Lady Ripon's letter). The Committee eventually decided 'with very much regret' that they were unable to respond positively. The President of the Infirmary had to explain that not only did the Constitution of the hospital not allow for the admission of wounded soldiers but that there was 'a large number of emergency and accident cases from Pits, Ironworks and other similar sources being dealt with; and at the same time the Committee had before them the stern fact that 620 civilians (were) awaiting admission'. Even two permanently occupied beds 'would mean depriving during the year between 20 and 30 civilian patients of the possibility of treatment'. It was never a question of finance but solely the duty which they had to their constituent population, and they were already taking 100 wounded soldiers and providing a further 100 beds on a temporary basis for the War Office.

Lord Dartmouth was disappointed at having to 'confess to failure' in a letter written to Lady Ripon on 28 August although he added that he was 'not without hope' and 'was not slacking off' in his attempts to increase bed provision. (His letterhead showed his telephone number to be the delightfully simple: Albrighton 12.)

Inevitably, there were many patients who, in spite of the care and attention which they received at the hands of the dedicated nursing staff, eventually died of their wounds. In fact, by 1917 a total of 615 men had died and it was felt that a memorial should be placed to them. Consequently, on 20 December 1917 in St John's Church, Waterloo Road, Queen Alexandra, accompanied by Princess Victoria, unveiled the memorial which was dedicated by the Bishop of Kingston, the Rt. Revd Samuel Taylor.

The introduction to the service recorded that the purpose was to 'render thanks to Almighty God for the service they have rendered, and for their willingness to offer their lives, to pray for a

7   *The Matron, Miss Davies (sixth from left), with three principal sisters and senior sisters*

merciful judgment on their sins, to entreat of our Heavenly Father a blessing on our land and our people, victory for the good cause, and the return of peace in our time'. Should some of these phrases sound quaint or judgmental, then another phrase will strike a similar note: 'That whatsoever defilements they may have contracted in this world through the lusts of the flesh or the wiles of the devil being purged and done away, they may enter into (the) eternal kingdom'. But however we may feel about the continuing changes of language, meaning and interpretation, the memorial itself and the intention of its founders speaks for the feelings of the nation which was holding in its prayers those who served and were serving in the theatres of war.

Writing in 1920, a civilian visitor to the Hospital, Mr. Allan White, who was to play a major part in voluntary service to the Hospital, recorded the impressions which he gained from his regular visits. He realised that, from the point of view of the patients, the hospital could appear to be a prison, something approaching heaven, or somewhere between the two. This really depended upon the state of health of the patient, and opinion would fluctuate. From the point of view of the outsider, the aspect which struck him most was the democratic nature of the establishment. By this he meant that the hospital was conducted entirely for the benefit of the patients, with no revenue accruing to the State in any way and with the staff receiving what might be termed a living wage, and not one which meant that they were profiteering. It was also democratic in the sense that it was a general hospital and so men with all kinds of injuries were treated in the same wards as those with organic troubles. As the war continued, this did change as there was inevitably a tendency to specialise. Whatever the reason for hospitalisation, though, when patients compared their injuries with those of their fellows, it was often the case that they realised that their own condition was not as bad as that of many others. (Similar observations are often made by those who come to Gifford House today for respite care or for convalescence. A study of the courage and cheerfulness shown by the long-term patients is often a significant learning experience.)

Mr. White noted, too, the absence of class distinction. In a ward of 60 men, some in bed, some in blues, nothing marked them out in terms of class, socially or professionally. Ambition had disappeared; men were no longer an engineer or a lawyer or even a soldier but a jaw, or head, or spine case.

This institution, with over two thousand people including patients and staff, created its own 'bond', which was influenced by the nature of the injuries, the length of time in the hospital and the problems associated with the men's futures. Nearly all were young and all were united by disability.

On first visiting the hospital he remembers feeling a sense of great depression at the sheer number and extent of the injuries received, but this was dissipated by the way in which he saw patients helping each other and the common sympathy which the patients had for their fellows. Pain, he felt, always present, was nevertheless a means of bringing men together in a self-supporting way and where, being so cosmopolitan, much advice and counsel could be given and received, not only in coping with pain and disability, but in planning for the future. Here life could begin afresh, the man of courage helping those with least and all of them proving that they were more than just 'men'.

This spirit played an important part, therapeutically, in the lives of the patients. This is perhaps a good point at which to look at their more personal needs, needs which could only be met by the voluntary provision of those items which make a time of hospitalisation a little more tolerable.

It is in that area that we shall discover the roots of what we know today as The Queen Alexandra Hospital Home for Disabled Ex-Servicemen.

CHAPTER 2

◆

LADY RIPON AND THE COMPASSIONATE FUND

The King George Hospital was established as a purely military hospital, even though a large number of civilians were on the staff. As such, the specification for equipment and the organisation of the hospital were on military lines, based on years of accumulated experience. The purpose of the hospital was that of all such hospitals: to return patients to active service as quickly as possible. The patient was first and foremost a soldier, and his regiment or unit needed him as an essential part of its operational capacity. Every soldier has a fund of regimental anecdotes and folklore, recounted at every reunion, which tell of the pressures firstly, never to report sick but, secondly, if that is unavoidable, when once having done so to return to the unit with all speed; in wartime this is particularly true.

However, the staff at the King George Hospital, along with the Joint Societies Committee and its supporters, quickly identified the need to enhance the basic (but nonetheless effective) medical care by the establishment of a Compassionate Fund and Gift Stores. The title might, at first sight, seem patronising and this was certainly a consideration at the time, for it was realised that it might give a wrong impression. But anyone who has served in H.M. Forces knows what is meant by 'compassionate', e.g. in the granting of compassionate leave; the meaning refers to a decision given or facilities granted which recognises the legitimate needs of an individual (as opposed to a unit) at a particular time in his service career.

The Compassionate Fund had a flying start with a donation of £1,030 cabled to the hospital by the Commercial Travellers' Association of Canada. Appeals were made for donations in cash and in kind, and a Gift Store was set up to handle the avalanche of gifts from an appreciative public; items would be purchased for patients if requests were reasonable.

The item most in demand was tobacco. It was felt that this was a great help to the soldier in a military hospital where smoking was permitted within reason at all hours of the day (modern medical staff might find this controversial). So the first stand-by of the stores was a plentiful supply of pipe tobacco, cigarettes and matches. Extras such as sweets were welcomed especially chocolate, bulls' eyes and 'acidulated drops', as were gifts of fruit, flowers and eggs. Toilet requirements were focused on replacing the standard Army issue items which had usually been lost during active service; shaving kit, toothpaste, brush and comb, personal aids, taken for granted by civilians, were given to the patients. Similarly, as most soldiers wish to write to their homes and loved ones, stationery and writing supplies formed another important element in the Gift Stores. As a traditional means of passing the time, a supply of reading material, especially short stories, was always on hand.

Each patient was provided by the Government with a blue hospital suit and red tie, but no other bedwear. So an appeal was made for articles of clothing:

Bed flannel dressing jackets	Dressing gowns
Day shirts	Large bed socks
Operation stockings	Operation gowns
'Helpless case' shirts	Vests

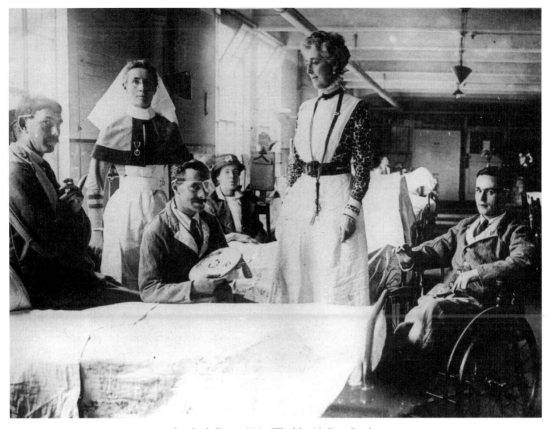

8 *Lady Ripon visiting Ward 2 with Sister Sparkes*

Several working parties were formed by friends of the hospital in south London to ensure a constant supply of garments. For the most suitable patterns, application was made to the British Red Cross offices in Pall Mall, and one can, in a flight of imagination, envisage a whole civilian army of seamstresses, needleworkers and machinists beavering away in respectable middle-class homes in the leafy suburbs! The temptation to caricature must be resisted, however, for the energy and enthusiasm of these voluntary workers served considerably to enrich the lot of the patient and to express the wish of many to minister to and support those who had risked their lives in the field of conflict. Today, we are often faced with refugee situations and appeals on similar lines and it is easy to imagine the willingness with which this request was met.

The Compassionate Stores and Gift Fund was under the control of Gladys, Marchioness of Ripon. This exceptional lady was to make her mark in this work and Gifford House was later to be founded in her memory. Her father was Sidney Herbert (1810-1861), 1st Baron of Lea. He was the second son of the 11th Earl of Pembroke by his second wife, the Countess Catherine, only daughter of Simon, Count Woronzoff, for many years Russian ambassador and for a long time resident in England. Herbert had a distinguished career, serving in the Cabinet under Peel, and later under Aberdeen as Minister of War and as Colonial Secretary under Palmerston. He was the mainspring of a Royal Commission on the sanitary condition of the Army, and took a leading role in the Army medical department, Army statistics and the Army school at Chatham. However, it was for his involvement in the conduct and consequences of the Crimean War that he made his name. Following the unacceptably high mortality rate and the lack of medical and hospital

9 *Lady Ripon at her desk (centre) with her team of helpers; Miss Phyllis Oakley-Williams (left) and Mrs. Hay seated in front of Lady Ripon with Mrs. Moore.*

facilities, underlined infamously at Scutari, Herbert devised a plan for a well-qualified friend of his to visit the Crimea, report and make recommendations. Her name was Florence Nightingale. We know that Herbert's daughter, Gladys, was acquainted with this famous lady and this is undoubtedly the source from which sprang her interest in military hospitals. Gladys' own daughter by her second marriage, Juliet, later recalled how she had to sit in a London cab while her mother visited Florence Nightingale—probably a frustrating event for the young girl. Gladys Herbert married the 4th Earl of Lonsdale and became Lady Ripon. After the death of the Earl, she re-married to Lord de Grey, when Juliet was four; Lord de Grey was an MP for a Yorkshire constituency. Lady Ripon was an enthusiastic champion of the Arts, especially ballet and the opera, and was influential in building contacts with Russian companies to perform in London. She saw the Diaghilev Ballet during a visit to Russia in 1909 and conceived the idea of bringing it to London for the Coronation of King George V. She was also a Lady-in-Waiting to Queen Alexandra. She was known for her beauty and striking personality. Disraeli once referred to her as 'the only woman I know who could revive the dignity and the fame of the political salon'. His analysis of character was correct though she had no taste for the theatre of politics. In an appreciation written after her death, Sir George Arthur wrote:

> She preferred to tread in further and broader, and perhaps straighter paths. She loved all that makes life beautiful; music and the drama and the colour and the travel, and above all—and perhaps because she loved these things—she loved humanity.
>
> Men and women of every class and creed came easily, and never came amiss to her. Each and all seemed to add something to the wide programme of her life; from her each and all received the sense of being welcome; each and all were infected with some of that spirit of joyousness which dominated her whole being and which nothing could quench or embitter.

In every capital of Europe, in every corner of England, in cottage or castle, the radiance of her presence shone out. Wherever she was, wherever she went, she contributed something—difficult to explain, impossible to forget.

Life was brimful of interest for her just because she could throw herself in all sincerity and with heart and brain into the interests of others. Life was for her a long progress of happiness, just because the happiness of others meant so much to her.

And then came the sudden, special call; the call perhaps for which she had unconsciously waited; the call she eagerly obeyed. England's honour had been at stake, and with something like fine recklessness England had flung herself into a fearful war—and a host of England's sons were stricken, and sorely hurt, and many were near to death. So Lady Ripon stood forward to take up the task which needed all her exquisite tact, her tireless energy, her knowledge of all that is good in the world, no less than the warmth of her brave heart.

This gifted and determined lady took over the running of the Gift Stores and Compassionate Fund and operated under rules laid down for its effective administration. The rules were published on 15 April 1915 and make interesting reading:

RULES FOR VISITORS AND GIFTS

1. The Gift Stores will be under the direction of the Marchioness of Ripon, as President of the King George Hospital Compassionate Fund, who will appoint her staff of voluntary assistants.

2. Issues to patients in Hospital of gifts from the Stores will be made on requisition of the Sisters in charge of the wards, under the supervision of the President, so far as the supplies available permit. The ward Sisters will, from time to time, be kept informed of the supplies available.

3. The distribution will be made by the ward Sisters, who will send a responsible person to collect the gifts and who will sign a receipt.

4. No worker, other than the President, or assistant deputed by her for the purpose, will be admitted to the wards, in connection with arrangements for visitors and gifts.

5. The Stores will be open daily for the issue of gifts, at such hours to be arranged, to suit the convenience of the Commandant and the honorary visiting staff.

6. All applications for appointments to visit the wards otherwise than for relations or personal friends of the patients, should be addressed to the Marchioness of Ripon. No visitor can be admitted to the wards without an appointment.

7. Visitors are requested to send gifts for distribution, not to individual patients, but to the Gift Stores. Lady Ripon will, however, give every possible consideration to the wishes of individual donors.

In case this seems rather formal, it must be stressed that the mood was one of care and thoughtfulness for the individual soldier. The rules ensured that the lines of communication were clear and Lady Ripon went about her task of enhancing the lot of those to whom she felt called to minister. They also ensured fairness, for it was a principle that all items were pooled, so that no one patient would be flooded with gifts while others were left out in the cold. Indeed, the Sister in charge of each ward would send to the Gift Stores a requisition sheet with the requirements for her particular ward. These demands were co-ordinated daily and made up as far as the stock in hand permitted.

An interesting letter to 'the lady readers of the *Times*' from Lady Ripon perhaps foreshadows what we would now term occupational therapy. She wrote asking for

a rather unusual object. The men in this hospital who are unable to get up naturally find the hours exceedingly long, and we have managed to interest a great many of them in needlework and embroidery. But alas! It is increasingly difficult, week by week, to procure materials for this work, and I have been wondering whether there are not a great many scraps of silk and wool, canvas, etc., which have been put aside, but which, collectively, would be of the greatest use to us here.

Perhaps the most valuable activity was the attempt to ensure that every soldier who was to be discharged was assisted in adjusting to his new conditions. In some respects, this was to foreshadow today's social service departments. A department was set up under the control of Mr. Allan V. White, whose impressions were recorded in the previous chapter, assisted by a clerk, a few lady helpers and a typist. When a patient had had his final Medical Board, the department got in touch with them, although in many cases they already knew them through the contacts established by the lady visitors on the wards. (These Medical Boards were critical in determining the future well-being of a patient, not least in financial terms.) Scanning the records of the war, one notices the extremely efficient system of Admission and Discharge books. These were initially completed whenever a soldier was first wounded; the book might be completed in a Field Ambulance under fire, in a Casualty Clearing Station or in a hospital. The system was so highly regarded for its accuracy and completeness that, if a book could not be found, the authorities assumed that it did not exist! This worked to the great disadvantage of the soldier, for upon him fell the onus to prove the extent of any incapacity. In the department, a system of record sheets and card indexes was set up giving the necessary personal details. The system enabled the staff to know where each man was, both physically and in terms of his approach to discharge. Thus patients who were released to the auxiliary hospitals were held on record so that they might nevertheless be helped. As someone wrote at the time:

> The men in the wards were constantly visited, so that we knew them all personally, and as any fresh facts were learned about a man the particulars were entered on his Record Sheet. We sought to be of service to these men in every way possible and they came to know that in any trouble that arose they could always find a kindly welcome and any necessary advice and help at our Office.

There was, however, some difficulty in gaining the confidence of the men, and some were definitely prejudiced against the office. Their fear was that the office would find them work to do which would thereby disqualify them for a pension (for which they were legitimately entitled). This was solved by the Army authorities issuing a leaflet which made it clear that any pensions to which they were entitled were guaranteed irrespective of any work a man might be able to do.

It is likely that over 10,000 men were helped in this way, and one can only imagine the correspondence which must have been generated with prospective employers. Many of those discharged were far from fit for work although healed of their disablement, and needed a period of recuperation and perhaps convalescent treatment before they were fit for work. Others had to try one job after another before they found something within their capabilities. One example was a man with hemiopsia, caused by a head injury which had destroyed one half of his field of vision. It took many months before a suitable job was found for him.

But it was claimed that whether or not everyone found employment, each patient who left was put in touch with someone in his neighbourhood who would assist and look after him. In the early days of the war, they were referred to the local 'Friends' of the Soldiers and Sailors Help Society, and then the Statutory Committees under the Naval and Military War Pensions Act, 1915.

This work was soon developed on a wider scale in order to meet needs which were not covered by the hospital. For example, many men suffering from head wounds had as a consequence lost the power of speech; teachers were obtained from some of the London County Council schools for the Deaf and Dumb to teach these men to talk again. One strange case was that of

> a man who had been severely wounded in the trenches and had fallen over the wire entanglements where he hung insensible, head downwards; he had an entire set of false teeth and these dropped out as he hung there. Because he had lost these and not had them shot out

of his mouth the Army while healing him of his wounds would not replace his teeth! We got in touch with the Ivory Cross people who did the necessary for him.

The men came to the department with all manner of worries. It might be about their treatment which they thought was retarding their recovery, there might be worries about their wives and families, about business matters and often money. This last anxiety was usually related to their pensions often concerning previous incomes. Some men had not made truthful returns of their income tax, others had enlisted under false names and worried about their pension entitlement when they returned home and would be known by their real names. One Irishman came to the office in great distress; he reckoned that he had a considerable amount coming to him but his statement showed only a very small amount. On taking the matter up, it was found that he had been debited with 'Separation Allowance to his wife' although he was a single man. Investigation showed that there was another man in his Regiment of the same name and almost the same Regimental Number, and the patient had been debited with the other man's wife's allowance.

Advice was also given on entitlement to disablement benefit. Thanks to their efforts, it was discovered that each disabled man was entitled to six months' benefit; a leaflet was prepared and advice given to some of the Societies who did not understand the regulations.

The soldier who was to be released into civilian life, being declared unfit for further service, lost his regimental links and friends. This could easily lead to a loss in confidence. One practical boost to his self-respect was to supplement the standard Government clothing issue on discharge. This had the particular benefit of adding to his acceptability when applying for a job. Good quality second-best suits, boots and shoes, ties etc. were all searched for in gentlemen's wardrobes in homes wherever the appeal made by the Stores became known. And if this does seem a strange way to support ex-soldiers compared with the raft of social service regulations and activity today, we must bear in mind that there have been many changes in perceptions over the years. One of the patients in Gifford House today,

10   *The Compassionate Stores. There are eggs, bulls' eyes and slippers on Lady Ripon's desk; the shelves are laden with clothing*

11 *A ward sister collects books and magazines, with Lady Ripon (right).*

Sidney Bristow, who grew up in Bermondsey, recalls some of the scenes from his young days:

> Wherever there was a busy thoroughfare or a market, like Jamaica Road or the Walworth Road, we would see groups of servicemen in uniform. There was usually a blind person, he'd have his hands on the shoulders of the man in front. There was always a limbless man on big wooden crutches or one who had lost an arm; they would walk in the gutter, with a tin begging bowl. Sometimes one might have a mouth organ, or they might be singing. They all seemed to be young, in their 20's. On the Brentford-Ongar road, there was a hospital where the grossly-disfigured were not even allowed out; half their faces might be missing – I remember them because my job was delivering potatoes to the hospital.

If a tradesman had lost the tools of his trade, these were supplied wherever possible, usually as the result of an appeal which Lady Ripon had made. The management of the Gift Stores must have been a complex business, bearing in mind the wide diversity of the items which they handled. Photographs of the time show the Stores and the team of volunteers. Amongst them was a Mrs. Verena Hay who was later to assume Lady Ripon's mantle and who witnessed at first hand the method and the vision of this remarkable lady.

Lady Ripon also controlled the handling of visits to the patients. The Matron, Miss M.E. Davies, wrote to a certain Miss Nicholson on 17 May 1915: 'the Marchioness of Ripon has very kindly undertaken the arrangements for visiting the Hospital, and application should be made to her'. Financial help was given to those families where there was extreme difficulty in paying fares in order to visit the hospital. The note throughout was one of care for the individual, and this thoughtfulness must have counted for much both to patient and family. In this aspect, the hospital owed a great deal to the hard work and dedication of the Chairman of its House Committee, Sir William Goschen.

One special group of visitors was given the warmest welcome on the first Christmas at which the Hospital was open. On Christmas Day, 1915, after services of Holy Communion at 6am, 8am and a Parade Service at 11am, the staff and patients prepared for the visit of members of the Royal Family. Each floor of the Hospital had its team of welcomers; Lady Ripon and Mrs. Hay were allocated the fifth floor. In the afternoon, King George V and Queen Mary, Their Royal Highnesses Princess Mary, Prince Henry and Prince George paid an informal visit. The Royal party spoke to every patient and all received a copy of Queen Mary's pale blue Gift-book. The effect of this must have been to boost morale considerably, and it is cause for much thanksgiving that the interest of the Royal Family has continued throughout the history

12 *Lady Juliet Duff (centre) with Sister Sparkes, Matron Davies (far right) and Mrs. Hay (extreme left).*

13 *An outing arranged by Capt. Cottle of the Church Army*

of Gifford House. Another aspect of the work of the Compassionate Fund, which had a small beginning but which turned out to be a major undertaking, was the arrangement of outings known as 'Joy Rides', a title which today seems somewhat anachronistic. These outings were arranged by Sir Arthur and Lady Wynne who found people willing to lend cars to take the convalescent patients for rides. This proved to be a great source of health and enjoyment and, when petrol restrictions were imposed, Sir Arthur arranged for the weekly hire of an omnibus or charabanc—either horse-drawn or with solid tyres! The pleasure which these rides gave to the patients was unquestionable. Friends showered invitations to tea, garden parties, concerts and other entertainments. On average, about 240 men each day enjoyed these outings; the organisation must have involved considerable time and energy. In fact, records show that by the end of 1916, 63,353 men had taken part in these 'Joy Rides'. One cannot help thinking that the military penchant for recording all movements and statistics had integrated itself in to the voluntary sector of this hospital! All these movements were in addition to the summer river trips which were organised with the support of the Port of London Authorities.

Additionally, there was the work to provide a regular programme of entertainments and concerts. This was supervised by Lady Tree. Offers were invited for the loan of 'six cottage pianos, for the duration of the war, for use in the patients' recreation rooms, and of any number of gramophones, with cheerful records'. She arranged, on average, four concerts per week. Her friends in the theatrical and musical circles rallied round to her support and apparently the audiences were both large and appreciative; some famous names were prominent in providing the entertainment.

The patients and staff also made their own entertainment, often producing shows in the day rooms. A programme still exists for a concert held on 20 June 1917. Written in black and red ink, it lists the artists, the sketches and the music. The programme notes refer, in a typical military style, to the non-availability of tobacco, the ill-fitting uniforms ('they only fit when they touch') and the standard of cooking. One notice reads:

> Patrons are requested to forward all deceased cats and dogs on Mondays and Fridays before 12 noon in future as we now have sausages for breakfast on Tuesdays and Saturdays!

But the lady behind this splendid organisation (which set standards of support and care for the whole person, since embedded in systems and principles of planning) was suffering herself from a terminal illness and a memorial service for Gladys, Marchioness of Ripon was held in St Margaret's Church, Westminster on 1 November 1917. Sir George Arthur wrote this tribute to her:

> Perhaps only those who came under her spell in that great Hospital, to which the Sovereign gave his own name, realize what was the worth of her work, and how she spent herself in it. And if she did much for the Hospital, the Hospital did much for her; for there she admittedly enjoyed the truly happiest days of her life. She spared nothing, reserved nothing, shrank from nothing, if only she might bring the hue of health, the taste of happiness, the hope of recovery, to the men she cared for and laboured for so wisely, so unostentatiously, and so well.
>
> And then she herself was stricken by pain—pain so grievous that those near her scarcely bore to think of it. She smiled at pain and knew no weariness in well doing, and when, all reluctantly as it would seem, Death came and touched her, she smiled at Death who could rob her of so little—and least of all, the affection of the soldiers she had tended in those last years.
>
> There are women—and Gladys Ripon was surely one of them—so buoyant in character, so quick and so constant in sympathy, so straight and strong in aim, that Death, whenever and however he comes, far from suggesting a term to beneficent activity, seems to point with sure finger to further employment in the spacious fields of a great hereafter.
>
> God rest her well and tell her, if it may be, that we miss her and love her, and would fain see her again. And let those who dwell in this Home dedicated to her memory see to it that they keep in fresh and sweet remembrance a brave, bright spirit which has fled a little way out of sight.

An obituary notice in the national press commented on her social graces and gifts which led her into acquaintance ranging from 'Empress to struggling artist. She was a friend of many artists—not only the successful ones. She and Lady Salisbury were the only two ladies invited by Lord Kitchener to Broome Park during the war'. The notice continues:

> When she took up her duties at King George's Hospital, until the last day of her illness eighteen months later, nothing was allowed to interfere with her work, and to her no event, public or social, compared in importance with the welfare of any individual at the hospital. During her illness Queen Alexandra went to see her nearly every day. Her death is a grievous event to many.

Not surprisingly, her many friends wished a memorial to be established in her name. Their wish was fulfilled less than two years after her death and one of her closest companions in the King George Hospital, Mrs. Verena Hay, to whom she bequeathed her diamond and ruby Red Cross brooch, was herself to be a living memorial through her own work for over 20 years.

CHAPTER 3

◆

Roehampton: The Opening Ceremony

What passing bells for those who die as cattle?
Only the monstrous anger of the guns
Only the stuttering rifles' rapid rattle
Can patter out their hasty orisons.
No mockeries for them; no prayers nor bells
Nor any voice of mourning save the choirs —
The shrill demented choirs of wailing shells;
And bugles calling to them from sad shires.

Wilfred Owen's poignant lines from *Anthem for Doomed Youth*, among many written as the Great War continued to take its toll, show a deep sense of frustration and anger, echoed in homes across the nation. Sapped by the bloodiest war in our history, there was a longing for peace but not without having discharged duty and obligation. So the wounded were cared for as newly-trained troops were drafted into Europe and a rugged determination showed in the face of everyone who had been affected by suffering or bereavement.

But the Armistice was eventually signed and the cost of war could be assessed. The sick and wounded reached proportions hitherto undreamed of, as demonstrated by these figures showing the number of sick and wounded arriving by year from the Expeditionary Force in France:

	Officers	Other Ranks
1914	2,660	66,626
1915	11,207	252,244
1916	26,360	496,793
1917	32,622	667,940
1918	36,542	640,008
1919	4,305	114,387
1920	145	7,057
Totals	113,841	2,245,055

(Source: *Medical Services General History: Vol. 1: Medical Services in the United Kingdom* by Sir W.G. MacPherson, HMSO, 1921, pp.372-3)

For the purposes of this history, the above statistics serve to illustrate the extent of the drop in demand for nursing care as the war came to an end, but the needs of those disabled in the war would remain for many years. The change of emphasis from purely surgical care to the continuing care of the disabled would be a new feature in the demand for medical services, both military and civil.

The King George Hospital was closed on 15 June 1919. They had admitted 70,504 patients, of whom 21,175 had suffered gunshot wounds. 10,812 operations had been conducted. The cost of salaries and wages during those four years was £107,398 8s. 9d. (over £4 million) with a fitting-up cost of £47,019 0s. 10d. (approaching £2 million). (Source: Reports by the Joint War Committee and the Joint War Finance Committee of the British Red Cross Society and the Order of St John of Jerusalem in England: On Voluntary Aid rendered to the sick and wounded at home and abroad and to British Prisoners of War, 1914-1919, with Appendices HMSO 1921.) The building was returned to civilian non-medical use, and it still stands, close to Waterloo Station, looking remarkably unchanged from the war years of 80 years ago.

The closure of the hospital was logical, but plans had to be made to care for the patients who still needed continuing treatment and whose discharge might be some time away. Reference has already been made to the auxiliary hospitals supporting King George's and we now focus on one of them—Gifford House. The name was pronounced 'Jifford' although it is now referred to with a hard 'G'.

The first recorded resident of this late 18th-century building in Roehampton was Andrew Berkeley Drummond, and then the Scottish poet, James Macpherson. The house became associated with the Gifford family, one of whom, Robert Gifford, was Attorney General in the same century. By 1894 it was the home of John Douglas Charrington of the brewery family. About 1905, he had the building extensively altered and a number of additions made. He did contemplate selling the house at one stage, but in fact offered it as a hospital for a period of 18 months. It was formally affiliated to the King George Hospital as an auxiliary hospital on 21 June 1915. Such hospitals were graded according to the facilities they provided, the skills of the trained staff and the level of equipment. Gifford House was given the top rating—A. The importance of this for the hospital

14   *Gifford House, Roehampton. There was a ramp from the house so that wheelchairs could reach the lawn and the summer huts outside the conservatory.*

itself lay in the capitation grant which the War Office would pay for each patient. In August 1914 this was 2s. per day, rising by a further 1s. three months later, and then 3s. 3d. in December, 1917 and, in the following month, 3s. 6d. Initially there were 140 beds but this number was increased to 190 a year later. At one time, during the height of the war, the number reached 230 beds. The government funding whenever local medical practitioners were employed was 4d. per bed per day for overseas cases and 3d. per day for cases transferred within the UK, subject to a maximum of 17s. 6d. and 12s. 6d. per week respectively.

Military discipline applied and the War Office issued 'Orders for Patients' (AFW 3114); they give the flavour of the day:

ADMISSION	Patients on admission will hand to the Pack Store Keeper the clothing and equipment they are wearing except the forage cap and boots. Articles such as razor, comb, hairbrush, toothbrush etc. will be retained for use in the ward.
WARD ROUTINE	All patients will obey the instructions of the Matron and the Nursing Staff, to whom they will always show due respect and afford every assistance. Patients who are NCO's will assist the Nursing Staff in maintaining good order and discipline. In the absence of a Member of the Nursing Staff the senior NCO present will be held responsible for any irregularity.
	Patients marked 'Up' will shave, wash, and dress before breakfast.
	Patients marked 'Up from—to—' will get up only for the times stated.
	If 'Up' they shall always wear their chevrons, and if confined to bed, their chevrons will be hung over their beds.
	Patients marked 'Up' will assist in such light duties in the Hospital as the Matron may direct.
	Patients will wear shoes in the building and boots in the grounds.
	Patients will not leave their wards till the termination of the MO's visit.
SMOKING	Smoking in the building is a privilege. Anyone found throwing used matches, cigarette ends etc. about the stairs or corridors will cause this concession to be withdrawn.
CORRESPONDENCE	All correspondence must be posted in the box provided. Letters must be left opened for the Censor.
COMPLAINTS	No complaint will be entertained unless submitted through the senior NCO in each Ward.

(Source: *ibid.*, p.214)

A Hospital Quartermaster was responsible for ordering supplies authorised by the Commandant and was also i/c the men's kits.

The duties of the Matron were also laid down. Whilst most of the specification refers to treatment and drugs etc., she was also to: 'Prevent waste and extravagance, both of food and also of dressings in the wards', 'Go round the wards at breakfast, dinner and tea, and see the diets are properly distributed and served' and to ensure staff were 'taught to cover carefully every scratch or sore on fingers or hands before doing dressings' (Source: *ibid.*, p.216).

Lady Juliet Duff had remained firmly interested in the work which her mother had begun. Early in 1918 she sent to Queen Alexandra a scheme to establish a convalescent home at Gifford House for soldiers discharged from the King George Hospital. The Queen thought that it was 'a splendid scheme and I shall be glad to Patronise it'. She felt that the Home should bear Lady Ripon's name 'as she really was its Founder and its President—and besides she thought and worried so much about the future of those brave wounded heroes'. Towards the end of April, Lady Juliet wrote again about the proposed name of the new Home and Queen Alexandra replied from Marlborough House:

> I received your kind letter a few days ago and although I would have preferred the Home for disabled Soldiers which was your mother's original idea to be called after her yet if you wish it give it my name and ADD In memory of your beloved Mother, its founder. That, I am sure, she would be pleased with.
>
> How one misses her more and more as days go on and I for one shall never cease regretting her untimely loss. I went the other day to have a look at her dear alas now empty house!—it gave me such grief and yet I was glad to see all the familiar and dear places both inside and outside the House!

(Lady Juliet wrote to her again in August, following the assassinations of the Russian Royal family. Queen Alexandra thanked Lady Juliet for her sympathy

> in my truly overwhelming grief about my beloved and miserable sister and the terrible and cruel fate which has befallen her and her poor children. The horrible murder of her loved and excellent [indistinct] save the poor young Emperor is too awful to think of … We are going to Sandringham next Saturday I hope as I feel half dead here in hot London and both Victoria and I want a little change. The world is full of sadness and misery wherever one looks although thank God we have been very lucky driving back those vile brutes of Huns.)

The full title was therefore agreed to be 'The Queen Alexandra Hospital Home for Discharged Soldiers In memory of Lady Ripon' and the formal opening took place on 9 July 1919.

The occasion was blessed with a day of brilliant sunshine and the front of the house was decorated with Allied flags, presenting a fitting background to the assembly.

Queen Alexandra arrived at 3.30pm and was received by the Chairman, Lady Juliet Duff, and the members of the Committee who conducted her to the platform in front of the house where patients, staff and friends had gathered. Miss Veronica Duff, a granddaughter of Lady Ripon, presented a bouquet to Her Majesty. Then a gift of £500 from the Abyssinian Government was presented to the Queen by Major Dodds, attached to the Abyssinian Mission, a gift that was greatly appreciated in the light of the heavy dependence on donations for the maintenance and further development of the Hospital.

The opening speech was made by Colonel Badeley, Chairman of the Executive Committee, who outlined the origins and objectives of the Hospital Home. He reminded the audience that the Scheme for the Home owed its initiation to the desire of the friends of the late Lady Ripon not only to set up a memorial to the splendid work which she had done but also to bring to fulfilment the work which she had so much at heart. He recalled the vivid memories which those who worked with her had of 'the wonderful fund of sympathy on which she was always drawing in regard to the men who came beneath her care, and her unswerving determination to leave no stone unturned to make for the happiness and welfare of these men'. She had always been conscious of the fear that adequate provision might not be made for those whose injuries were such that 'time would not dim their suffering'.

As the result of the Scheme which the Committee had put forward, a considerable sum of money had been subscribed by the friends of Lady Ripon, and grants had been received from the Finance Committee of the British Red Cross Society and Order of St John of Jerusalem. He also paid tribute to the generosity of Mr. and Mrs. Charrington who had lent the house in 1915 and had extended the lease until 1920. (This statement was welcomed by a round of applause.) He

15 *Queen Alexandra speaking at the Opening Ceremony; Lady Juliet Duff is on her right.*

hoped, he said, by that time to be in a position to buy a permanent home. To that end, further subscriptions would be invited and probably the Committee would be writing a letter asking for further and larger subscriptions. He did think that a certain sum of money on balance from the old Hospital might be at their disposal.

Colonel Badeley paid tribute to the tireless energy of Mrs. Hay who had succeeded Lady Ripon in her work. Mrs. Hay had continued in the same spirit which Lady Ripon had set as an example, and she had shown that she was fired by an ambition to bring her predecessor's work to a perfect conclusion.

Addressing the Queen, he thanked her for graciously consenting to allow her name to be used in connection with the Hospital Home and that was an indication to the world 'of the character we wish this Hospital Home to bear'. Although the Ministry of Pensions had taken over a stupendous work in caring for those who had been injured in the War, the purpose of the Home was to bring to all the patients 'the human touch of personal sympathy and individual help' which even the most efficient organisation could not always bring; the experience of the King George Hospital had shown how vital it was to the success of an enterprise of this kind both for those who had been paralysed and for those whose injuries were not so severe.

Lady Juliet Duff, Lady Ripon's daughter, then asked Queen Alexandra to declare the hospital open, and this was Her Majesty's reply:

> It gives me the greatest pleasure to open this Hospital Home in memory of my dearest friend
> Lady Ripon who worked so hard for all of you. I wish every success to the Hospital Home,

and I would like to thank Mr. and Mrs. Charrington for their kindness, and the Abyssinian Government for having given us this beautiful large sum.

The modern reader may conclude that Her Majesty was sparing in her use of words. But quantity is never the best measure of attitude and everyone at Gifford House knew of the keen and long-lasting interest which she had in its welfare. Indeed, her thoroughly positive interest was shown that very day when later she inspected the hospital and spoke to some of the patients. A record of those conversations stated that she won 'the hearts of all by the sympathetic interest she took in their condition and the cheery way in which she wished them a speedy recovery'. That attitude continued to shine through strongly in the interest taken by her successors.

The Revd J. Gough McCormick then said a prayer of Dedication which was followed by a speech by the Minister of Pensions, who was specially charged with the care of the disabled. After thanking the Queen for her continuing interest, and the Committee and subscribers who had made the establishment of the Hospital Home possible, he took up the point made by Colonel Badeley about the necessarily limited role of the Government. 'The State has the special duty of looking after the disabled men, but its work must necessarily be mechanical as it must deal with the average rather than the special cases'. He admitted that however well Government departments might carry out their responsibilities, it was quite impossible for them to cover the difference between State and private management—the institution and the home. The reason for this Home's existence was that it was wanted, but the State was able to make more liberal provision in special cases. He said: 'Thirty three shillings a week is not really a fair summary of what is done for the totally disabled, and the Home could only be maintained day by day if the State made a considerable provision for the patients in the Home'. The State did deduct 1s. a day from a man's allowance, but for that sum of 7s. a week it was paying out nearer 70s. a week when he was being maintained in the Home. The Minister realised quite well that much more had got to be done than any State institution could do. (This is a theme which is a continuing feature of our social economy viz. the demand for services will always outstrip the finance available. Effort will always be called for to augment State aid, and this is still true of Gifford House, however social support payment systems may have been upgraded. Opportunities for individual service and commitment are still there for our response, as were the challenges which the first Governors faced.)

16 *Lord Ripon speaking at the Opening Ceremony. Apart from his political interests, he was a keen collector of Dresden china and enjoyed field sports. A list he signed in 1921 shows a total of over 500,000 game, hares and rabbits killed in 44 years, plus two rhino, 11 tigers and 12 buffalo.*

Sir Arthur Stanley then spoke on behalf of the British Red Cross Society. He carried a message from Sir Douglas Haig expressing his regret for being unable to attend. Sir Arthur praised the Field Marshal for the vigorous action he had been taking with the Ministry of Pensions on behalf of those who had received such disabling injuries in the war (this evoked a round of applause from the company). He felt quite certain that a combined effort from the Ministry of Pensions and the British Red Cross would ensure that sufficient money would be forthcoming for the upkeep of the Hospital; everyone wished it to be kept up in memory of Lady Ripon who had been one of the first to come forward when the war broke out in 1914.

He said that it was interesting to remember that the first thing she did for the Red Cross was to go on a mission to France, for which her intimate knowledge of the country and the people well qualified her. Largely due to that visit, relations with the French Red Cross had been most harmonious. It was Lady Ripon who first had the idea of sending out parcels to combatants and prisoners of war, 'but it was not until the King George Hospital was started that Lady Ripon found her true vocation' and one of the first letters received from Queen Alexandra expressed the wish that Lady Ripon should be associated with the Hospital. The war had come to an end but the good work of that Hospital must not die as the result of the signing of the peace. 'The result has been the foundation of this institution here which is to look after the men whose interests Lady Ripon had so deeply at heart'. Every bed in the King George Hospital had been endowed, and agreement had been given for them to be transferred to Gifford House—a link which would keep alive her memory. He ended on a poignant note: 'The last time I saw Lady Ripon, not long before she died, she was in great pain and suffering but she felt that her sufferings were slight in comparison with others'.

The concluding speech was made by the Marquis of Ripon. He thanked Queen Alexandra for so graciously attending. She had endeared herself to the whole nation by the keen and kind interest which she had shown in the Hospitals and in

> the gallant men who fought so nobly for their King and Country in this long and terrible War. I thank you for what you have said of my wife and of what she has done. It is not for me to praise my dear wife's work, but I know that she strived her utmost to do her duty and she stuck to her post until illness and suffering made it impossible for her to go on. While she was ill in her room her heart was still in the King George Hospital, and she was always asking how

17   *Queen Alexandra meets some of the patients. The wheelchair is chain-driven.*

the work was going on in the Department over which she presided, so ably assisted by Mrs. Hay. It is a consolation to me to know how much her work was appreciated. If you cast a stone into a calm lake, ripples will run along the surface. My wife has gone, but the ripples of her memory still remain.

An emotional and heartfelt expression of the contribution of Lady Ripon thus brought the formal aspect of the Opening Ceremony to an end. Queen Alexandra then made an inspection of Gifford House.

A musical performance was provided by the band of H.M. Royal Horse Guards (Blues) and Dame Nellie Melba sang. Amongst the musical items were a Processional March by Bilton dedicated to Field Marshal Sir Douglas Haig and Elgar's *Land of Hope and Glory* sung by Cpl. Wornell. The invited guests enjoyed a tea, and after Her Majesty had left, were then able to inspect the House themselves.

Fortunately, the ripples which the Marquis described have indeed continued to make themselves evident throughout the subsequent history of Gifford House and it is entirely fitting that the marble bust of Lady Ripon by Antonin Carles, dated Paris 1886, should still grace the entrance hall today.

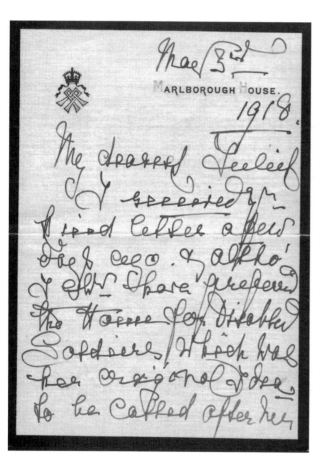

May 3rd

My dearest Juliet,

I received your kind letter a few days ago and although I would have preferred the Home for the disabled Soldiers which was your mother's original idea to be called after her yet if you wish it give it my name and ADD In Memory of your beloved Mother, its founder.

18 *Queen Alexandra's letter in which she agreed to the Home being named after her.*

CHAPTER 4

◆

THE NURSING SCENE

People are the lifeblood of any organisation. As we explore the history of this remarkable institution, we shall become acquainted with some outstanding personalities and with people devoted to the welfare of the patients. We begin by looking at the nursing scene. Here is the very heart of the hospital where the care is given to a wide range of patients. Characters begin to emerge and so we can glimpse the relationships which were so important in every aspect of patient care.

One patient of those far off days, 3/7888 Cpl. William Lunn, MM, who celebrated his 100th birthday on 15 December 1996, recalls his time at Gifford House:

I went to Gifford House in 1918. I had served with the 6th Bn The Yorkshire Regiment in Gallipoli (1915) and then on the Somme, where I was wounded and lost the lower half of my left leg. I was sent to Queen Mary's Hospital, Roehampton in 1917, who passed me on to Gifford House while a wooden leg was being made for me. I seem to recall that I was one of about 40,000 soldiers who required similar aids during the war. Gifford House was in what was then called 'Millionaire's Row'. The house belonged to Mr. J.D. Charrington of the brewery firm. The house was in its own grounds, with a bowling green at the back and the whole surrounded by cypress trees.

As a patient, I was warded on the ground floor, in the magnificent ballroom with its beautiful glass chandeliers. The paraplegic patients were on the first floor. We all wore uniform—blue outer suit, grey shirt, red tie, regimental hat and badge. The uniform jacket had to be clay-piped white on the lapels each day.

The Matron was a Miss Pollock—big, strict but fair. Patients' dressings were attended to by the female VAD staff, the male orderlies covering the manual work, cooking etc. We had three meals a day; the standard breakfast was one hardboiled egg, with a hunk of bread and

19 *Mr. William Lunn in his 100th year accompanied by his daughter and fellow Green Howard Leslie Gunn.*

margarine. The other meals were usually stew and dumplings or boiled beef. Each patient provided his own knife, fork and spoon as we were still serving soldiers and this was part of our kit.

We had no pay or money; it was all sent to our next-of-kin and my mother used to send me money from the allowance paid to her. Mr. Charrington would visit us, arriving in a smart hansom cab with his footman. Mr. Charrington was plainly dressed, often in an old coat, and would give each patient one cigarette.

Those of us who were able would head for London after breakfast. The favourite place was Hyde Park where we would listen to the band—and hopefully receive the odd hand-out. The clippies on the buses always let us travel free.

Gifford House was run on service lines for discipline and routine. We had to be back by 1900 hours. Many who were late climbed in over the fence—legless or not. Our excuses for being late were—missed the last bus, had to walk back, lost my money, got lost. I was caught more then once—and sent back to Roehampton as punishment but they did not have room for me and so I returned to Gifford House.

We have a wonderful record of the day-to-day life of Gifford House in the pages of *The Gifford Journal* or, to use its sub-title, the *House Magazine of the Queen Alexandra Hospital Home, Roehampton, for Discharged Soldiers*. The first edition was published in December 1919, Mrs. Hay providing the finance for its printing. The emphasis was on reporting often with humour the events and happenings of the hospital. We shall be drawing on this journal for the years up to 1933 when it ceased publication on the move to Worthing. The articles were written by patients, staff and visitors; the editors varied as patients arrived and left but one thing is quite clear—the matron had

20   *Miss Pollock, Matron, with a group of sisters*

a strong censorship role! That being said, the style of the reporting and the range of topics gives a splendid panorama of daily life.

Before we explore that avenue, it will be helpful to get a flavour of the kind of publication it was. First, it had a definite sense of its own value, for Mrs. Hay sent copies of the first issue to both Queen Mary and Queen Alexandra, and the gracious replies received from Buckingham Palace and Sandringham were no doubt welcomed.

Some of the earlier contributors were from outside and one of the more famous names was that of Hilaire Belloc. This was due to the efforts of Lady Juliet Duff, the daughter of Lady Ripon. (We shall be referring to her by this name throughout this history. She first married Robin Duff who was killed in the First World War; she later remarried and was known as Lady Juliet Trevor but, following a divorce, resumed her name of Duff.) Lady Juliet, finding her contacts with her literary friends proving to be somewhat jejune, finally 'captured Mr. Belloc, told him that his new book of verse and his proofs for *The New Statesman* must go uncorrected until he had written something for a far more im-

"AM I DESCENDED FROM A MONKEY, AUNTIE?"
"I DON'T KNOW DEAR, I NEVER KNEW ANY OF YOUR FATHER'S PEOPLE."

21 *Drawn exclusively for the Gifford Journal by G.L. Stampa, the artist from* Punch

portant and widely read Journal, and he was not to leave the writing table until he had finished'. The result was an epitaph 'On the Dead Dog of a Politician' and this epigram:

> Mary had a little lamb,
> For which she didn't care a damn:
> And yet the lamb was so contrary,
> It ceased at last to care for Mary.

Other contributors were from *Punch*, among them Max Malini, Bert Thomas and G.L. Stampa who produced a delightful cartoon (see plate 21).

One poetic contribution was, sadly, anonymous:

> There was a pious young priest
> Who lived almost wholly on yeast;
> For he said: "It is plain
> We must all rise again—
> And I want to get started at least!"

In June 1921, the *Journal* was obliged to become self-financing and so advertisements appeared, mainly from local suppliers such as the Hogarth Laundry, the Roehampton Motor Co. (cars for hire by the hour or day, any make supplied, for early trains, theatres, country runs), and W. Powley & Son, Bootmakers, who were agents for Lotus, Delta and Phat-Pheet (!) shoes. Harrods also advertised; one advertisement merely says: 'Get it at Harrods Ring SLOANE 1234' where a Combination Bedstead cost £2 19s. 6d., a divan eight guineas and a 12ft x 9ft carpet £9 12s. 0d.

To return to personalities. The first Matron of Gifford House was Miss L. Pollock but the first issue of the *Journal*, in December 1919, begins with a farewell to her. Miss Pollock had been at Gifford House for four years, that is to say when it was an Auxiliary Hospital and often received patients from the King George Hospital. She had therefore been involved in a nursing operation which had had to cope with the unprecedented high number of casualties from the First World War. This clearly had demanded much of anyone in the nursing field and the note in the *Journal* states that four years of strenuous war work had left her feeling the need for a change. Miss Pollock probably felt that it was preferable to let the new management team set up its own nursing systems; if so, that was a perfectly understandable attitude. She decided to follow her profession abroad. She left with some glowing comments: 'The best wishes of all the House go with her; we find it difficult to imagine the hospital without her; the excellent discipline which has been maintained, at the same time allowing a maximum amount of freedom has made us realize the meaning of the term "Hospital Home"'.

That was praise indeed from patients and Miss Pollock had begun a tradition which still pervades the Worthing home. She wrote a letter from Los Angeles in the following January, thanking everyone for her 'beautiful present' and recounting how the Atlantic crossing had been rough but that Christmas in Philadelphia had been ideal. She travelled south to New Orleans where 'the season changed to summer'. She had taken the *Sunset Express* for the 5,000-mile journey to Los Angeles, leaving a dry and dusty Arizona and arriving in Southern California 'where everything looks green. I never saw such a change. It is the most beautiful country in the world'.

She goes on: 'I saw carnations selling at a cent each today, which is a half-penny in England … I am thoroughly enjoying it and so would you boys. I only wish you had a little of this lovely sun … I must close with best wishes to all the Boys, and trust that 1920 will bring you the best of good luck and good health', doubtless a wish that was heartily reciprocated.

Miss Pollock's successor was Miss Harte who, by February, had 'already endeared herself to everyone in the hospital'. The *Journal* went on to say that 'we hope she will not be embarrassed when we say that she has achieved a high state of popularity, which we have not the slightest doubt she will keep'.

Miss Harte wrote an article for the *Journal* about her nursing experience in the Navy before the War; it gives an interesting insight into the practices of the day:

> Nursing in the Navy is carried out by the Sisters and the Sick Berth Staff. The former consists (at the three large hospitals—Haslar, Plymouth and Chatham) of a Head Sister, a Superintending Sister, and a number of sisters according to the size of the hospital. Their President is Queen Alexandra and they wear her badge (her monogram with crown, Geneva Cross, anchor and cable).
>
> The sick berth staff consists of one Head Ward Master; Ward Masters in number according to size of hospital; first and second-class stewards; sick berth Attendants and Probationer sick berth Attendants. Special attention is paid to the training of these men who are recruited at all three large hospitals. There is a staff of Masseurs to instruct them in massage and an instructor from the National School of Cookery comes to each hospital for a month every quarter. Lectures are given by the Surgeon-in-Charge, the Dispenser, and the Instructing Sister. There is also a Drill Sergeant.
>
> During the war nearly all the permanent staff went to ships and hospital ships and were replaced by the Q.A.R.N.N.R. Sisters and the St John Ambulance men of whose work too much cannot be said. The blue jacket is an ideal patient, rivalling in pluck and cheeriness his brother of the 'sister service'.
>
> As I have now had the privilege of knowing both sailor and soldier patients, I have, after deep deliberation, decided that 'both are best'. We had three hundred Army patients—officers and men—after the first battle of Ypres, as our wards were fairly empty at the time and the military hospitals were full to overflowing. When we had to part it was with mutual regrets.

We had large numbers of (the) Naval Brigade from the Dardanelles, many of them in a pitiable state with dysentery, and also men from the Jutland Battle, mostly suffering from severe scalds and burns. In spite of their suffering they were all full of pride at the drubbing they had given the enemy.

Clearly a lady with considerable nursing experience, and also with diplomatic awareness, yet in March 1921 the editor of the *Journal* bemoans her departure which had come as a disappointment to the Hospital:

Besides losing a Matron we are also saying good-bye to a very dear friend, for in the twelve months that the Matron has been with us she has shown herself so keenly interested in all pursuits and activities of the men, and so ready to help that her departure will be felt everywhere, while her kindly sympathy will be missed by many who had found her on numerous occasions a friendly listener. That she had become attached to us all, we know, for were we not honoured on one occasion by being compared with her former patients from the Navy?

Miss Harte had certainly lived up to her name and, from the patients' point of view, it does seem that she had been a popular Matron and was a loss to the hospital. There is a suggestion, however, amongst the ranks of the Governors that Miss Harte was probably not the best appointment which they had made, turning out to be a harsh disciplinarian and, in the opinion of some, not up to the requirements of the post (which had been so predicted by someone involved in her selection). Be that as it may, she was to be excelled in the popularity stakes by her successor, Miss L. Fletcher, about whom there was never any doubt concerning her competence and effectiveness.

Miss Fletcher, whose name was Lizzie but who was known as Beth, was a Ward Sister at Gifford House when it opened; in appointing her, the Committee had the distinct advantage of knowing her work and her dedication at first hand. She had trained at the Bolingbroke Hospital which was affiliated to St Thomas' Hospital in London. After joining the Queen Alexandra's Imperial Military Nursing Service, she went as a Ward Sister to the King George Military Hospital in charge of the Paraplegic Ward. She was then 28. The majority of her patients had suffered spinal injuries as a result of gun shot wounds and had had long and extremely uncomfortable journeys back to England from France. The death rate was very high. She had asked many times to be posted to France where she felt she could be of more use. The Matron, Miss M.E. Davies, refused her request each time, telling her that she was needed where she was. The Consultant Physician Dr. (later Sir) E. Farquhar Buzzard heard of these requests and asked her why she wanted to leave the ward. When she explained that she felt she did not know enough about the treatment for paraplegics, he replied: 'None of us do, but we need you to help us find out'. So she remained at the Hospital where she first had contact with Lady Ripon and Mrs. Hay.

22 *Miss Beth Fletcher, ARRC, Matron*

Many years later, the Chief Executive of Gifford House, Miss J. M. Holgate, recalled how Miss Fletcher spoke of those days in the Military Hospital:

> One could feel that she still had a vivid picture of so many helpless cases for which so little could be done, and she could still hear the distressing sounds which came from the wards treating those with head injuries. At the same time she told many tales of the wonderful spirit of comradeship and fun which the young servicemen shared with the staff. There was a feeling, too, of the civilian support for nurses in uniform; bus conductors rarely collected fares and they were made to feel special wherever they went when they were off duty.

Gifford House had certainly appointed someone special. Miss Fletcher served as Matron for 38 years, finally retiring from Worthing in 1959.

The editor of the *Gifford Journal* in 1921, F. Dawson, was definitely a 'fan' of the new Matron. There are cynics among us who say that the good things about people are only said at the time of their funeral, but Mr. Dawson wrote a panegyric about the new Matron which turned any such criticism on its face. He speculated on the reasons for her popularity:

> Is it because we know that our Matron, previous to her recent appointment, made such a study of the nature of the disability which has left us in hospital that she was able to deal with it in every condition, and that we have, therefore, at hand always someone who could understand how we feel?
>
> Partly, perhaps, but not entirely, because I am quite sure myself that the study of paraplegia on the part of our Matron has been done purely for the benefit of the paraplegic himself and not in the least with a view to her own promotion.
>
> Even that is not all. Besides the physical condition, she has made a study of the minds of men like the Giffites. [This was the affectionate nickname given to the patients and to which they are often referred in the *Journal*, the 'G' being pronounced as a 'J'.] She knows how to amuse them; she is an expert in the art of teaching them how to occupy their minds to the exclusion of anything in the nature of brooding or worry. Their pastimes are hers; she can discuss with them whatever they are interested in, in a way that shows a knowledge of the subject by no means casual. She can enjoy a joke with anyone (I myself have seen her pitch a rolled up towel at an apple balanced on a patient's head in imitation of William Tell), while an appeal to her sympathy never finds her wanting.

That, he felt, was one of the reasons why discipline depended very little on hard and fast rules.

Mr. Dawson decided to interview the Matron. To his first question as to what she thought of spine cases, Miss Fletcher replied: 'The more I see of them, the more I am determined that I will remain with them'. She told him about her training years and about her involvement in the Entertainments Committee of the Bolingbroke Hospital, which covered a variety of social activities, the most dramatic of which was arranging a roller-skating evening on the roof of the hospital! The authorities intervened, explaining that the noise 'would not be beneficial to the more serious cases'.

Her years at the King George Hospital were summed up briefly:

> I went to the King George Hospital in June 1915. As you know, the top floors were opened first and the others staffed as soon as they were ready. I went into the first floor and we anxiously waited for the first convoy. Things soon got very busy after that.
>
> In June 1916 I went into M.1, which was then the paraplegia ward. In the winter of that year, however, we removed into C.D.1 on account of the cold—beds, patients, trollies, everything. I remained with the paraplegics until K.G.H. closed in 1919 and of course except for two short periods, have been with them here. Also as I told you before, to remain with them a long time yet is my most sincere desire.

That desire was to be fulfilled to the benefit and gratitude of countless patients who found themselves in the care of such a dedicated lady.

That dedication, which had already shown itself in her career so far, was recognised in a very tangible way when she was invested as an Associate of the Order of the Royal Red Cross. The account of this event was recorded in the *Gifford Journal*:

> On July 19th the curiosity of the Giffites was aroused by seeing two figures in the well-known uniform of the Military Nursing Service, and another one in the equally well-known one of the British Red Cross Society, being hurriedly ushered out into a waiting car. It was only when the car returned some two hours later, that we learned the cause of the sudden reappearance of these uniforms so reminiscent of the war. Matron, Sister Hulbert and Sister Murrell had been received at Marlborough House by Queen Alexandra, and presented by her with a book and picture which is given to all who have been invested with the Order of the Royal Red Cross. Matron and Sister Hulbert were invested with the Order two years ago, and Sister Murrell was gazetted last year, but none of them had been fortunate enough to be among the ladies received by Queen Alexandra. Mrs. Hay, knowing this, kindly arranged to obtain permission for them to be received whenever Her Majesty was receiving other Members of the Nursing Service. Queen Alexandra takes a great interest in the Hospital Home which bears her name, and made several enquiries regarding the patients and said that she hoped to visit them again shortly and hear more of all they are doing.

(That was a wish which she was able to fulfil as we know from the details of her visits.)

Many of the personalities of the nursing staff remain unnamed, although we shall meet Sisters Hulbert and Murrell again, both of whom gave long service. The whole tenor of the *Gifford Journal* is one of appreciation of the nursing staff coupled with a healthy badinage. Personalities there most definitely were. For example, one of the nursing staff was very short in stature and was referred to as the 'Little One'. A certain 'W.J.B.' wrote a 14-verse poem about the trials this nurse experienced when trying to manoeuvre one of the patient's wheelchairs in the restricted space of the ward. She did not realise that the brake was on; when the patients finally decided to tell her, she then had to move a bed and then a locker to achieve enough space for the turn. Patients came from other wards to see what the fuss was about, and this only added to her embarrassment. They made such helpful comments as:

'You are so small, you cannot see
Over the top', they cried in glee.
'A paper spread upon the floor
Would raise you, then, you could see o'er.'

The 'Little One' eventually enlists the help of an orderly and flees in confusion ...

A visitor to Gifford House, a former nursing Sister, writing a few months later, recounted how 'a certain sergeant in a certain intellectual ward' had said to her: 'We had a member of staff who was very small, but she added two inches to her height by attending the gymnasium daily, and hanging on the bar'. She handed this advice on gratuitously to the poor 'Little One' whose wail she had read, in the hope that it might prove a help to her. A cartoon appeared to illustrate the difficulties of this nurse (see plate 23).

It would not have been surprising if the nursing staff did at times find the humour of

23   *Trials of a Little One*

the patients exasperating but there is no evidence of any malice in their intentions. The staff were probably able to see the funny side of things. For example, a member of staff recorded for the *Journal* the following story:

> Picture a ward of 33 patients in a large military hospital, a poor night sister striving to subdue the exuberant spirits and chattering tongues of many of the boys who are well on the road to recovery and strongly object to 8pm bedtime. She has used all her persuasive powers and expects every moment to see the Night Sister at the door to reprimand her for not keeping better order. As usual there are so many things to be told at this hour (there having been no time during the day!).
>
> This particular evening they are worse than usual, and the Sister, becoming desperate, exclaims, 'Oh! if only I had dumb patients!'
>
> The following evening the Night Sister, on receiving the report from the Day Staff, is told they have had a convoy of one—a very bad head case with terrible wounds, high temperature, and not expected to live through the night. Suddenly there is an agonising cry of 'Sister! Sister!' and all eyes are turned towards the new patient. The Sister dashes towards his bedside, the rest of the ward looking on with pleasurable anticipation. Nothing can be seen of the patient but bandages as he is lying well under the bedclothes. 'What is the matter, old man?' asks the Sister, placing her hand lightly on his shoulder and commencing to move away the clothes. Suddenly she springs back—there are roars of laughter from the patients, one of whom cries out, 'A dumb patient for you, Sister!'

There is a tradition amongst all nursing staff, one suspects, that they are always in the right; that, at least is sometimes the impression which they like to give, or which patients perceive. If one such cocksure nurse was of that belief, then we should find no difficulty in understanding how the patients felt one brilliant moonlight night in 1921 when a new nurse came on duty. Armed with a coal bucket and shovel, she asked the patient in the end bed to direct her to where in the grounds she could find the hut containing the heap of coke, the fuel for its stoves. (A salutary reminder of very different heating systems and of the physical demands on the nursing staff.) After giving careful instructions, the patient offered her the use of his cycle lamp 'to be on the safe side'. 'Lamp!', said the nurse contemptuously, 'on a night like this! Oh, no, I can manage perfectly well without a lamp, I'm sure.'

Fifteen minutes later she returned, bringing a well-filled bucket. 'There', she exclaimed breathlessly, 'I told you I wouldn't be long, and as you see I didn't need a lamp.' The patient carefully examined the bucket. 'I don't know. This isn't coke, it's clinkers.' For once a nurse was discovered at a loss for words.

One of the patients at this time was inspired to write about the nursing staff. 'J.M.' entitled his piece: 'The Nurse-Bird. An Essay on a New Species'.

> The Nurse bird may be described, usually, as a town bird. It has, however, been seen very frequently in the country, especially in the larger villages, but has never been known to stop there if it could fly to town. During the last four or five years its numbers have increased enormously but before this it was comparatively rare. The plumage of the bird is mainly white, with grey wings and tail, the wings being sometimes marked with red or white stripes and tipped with white. Usually it has a peculiar red mark shaped like a cross just beneath the head. The nest is always built inside the house and the bird has a decided preference for top floors. It seems to have no particular time of rest for it is to be seen flying about at all hours of the day and night. The bird has very neat and tidy habits. Anything in the way of dust or old papers left about seems to incite it to fury, and articles on the locker tops have the same effect unless they are few in number and tidily arranged.
>
> The species is very interested in needlework and photography and seems very pleased when it is having its picture taken. The science of this hobby also seems to interest the bird for it has been seen in the Dark Room at lectures. Nothing definite can be said about the food

which these birds eat as it seems to vary a good deal with the seasons. It has, however, a decided preference for chocolates all the year round and ice-cream in the summer. The Nurse bird is apparently very fond of company and has been known to keep pace with people for miles. It is rarely seen alone, but generally flies about in small groups, the usual number being two or three.

It would be interesting to know how many of today's nursing staff would claim to recognise this species!

Some of the nursing staff established a special rapport with the patients. For example, when Sister Bush resigned in 1921 there was genuine sorrow at her departure. It was said that she had never been obtrusive but had always been at hand when required, and her capability was unquestioned. She had confessed to her happiest times being spent with 'the boys', first at the King George Hospital but chiefly at Gifford House.

One of the so-called 'joys' which the patients had to endure was that of spring cleaning and sometimes re-decoration. The patients' view was that the nursing staff were too zealous in their activities. Once the ward had been re-decorated and the painters had departed, the patients are moved back and the 'nurses have their turn and start avenging their past wrongs on the lockers'. A patient puts up a plea: 'Have you ever gone to your locker to find anything in a hurry after a nurse has cleaned out the drawers? If you do not take all the things out to find the object of your search the last one you remove, the nurse would consider she had failed miserably with your locker and do it all over again when you had gone out'. Then their attention is turned to other things. Everything to be scrubbed is scrubbed hard and put out to dry. The patient is told to go out; he steers through all the bed-tables and chairs and finally manages to reach the lawn where he is thankful to know that when he returns, the spring-cleaning will be over for another year!

Odd little snippets occur which make us wish that we knew just a little more. Who was the Sister who had a cat which was 'recently the subject of a song by a well-known artiste' (and apparently was introduced to him and made a great impression upon him)? What was the origin of 'Here is the little Red Book, Sister'? What did nurse T mean when she said that it was 'easier now to be good than it used to be'? And what was it that caused one of the Sisters to be overheard stating that she had discovered, after careful search, the 'footprints of an unseen hand'?

And the male nurses also came into the reckoning. One record exists of a conversation between a patient and a male nurse on one of the wards:

Male Nurse.   Now B, are you ready?
B(a patient)   Yes, chum.
M.N.   Please don't be so familiar. I expect more politeness from you. Are you ready for me?
B   Yes, old bean.
M.N.(growing heated)   That's worse, and I won't have it.
B   Then what must I call you? What are you? 'Nurse' or 'Male Nurse'?
M.N.   I'm a nurse, obviously male. So call me 'Nurse!'

One male orderly at least must have wondered about the thinking processes of the patients, one of whom had recently acquired a motorised chair. The patient was seen to strike a match to enable him to see into his petrol tank. The male orderly rushed to his aid, only to be told: 'It was alright, I was using a safety match'!

Amongst many patients who spend time under the supervision of nursing staff there is usually an admiration for the work they do and some such patient in Gifford House was able to pen this short verse:

The Perfect Nurse

Take an oceanful of energy
A tablespoon of guile,
About a quart of innocence
A little less of wile;
A pinch or two of naivete
A touch or so of nerve,
A hamperful of courage
And just twice as much of verve;
A large amount of sweetness,
And a sprinkling of conceit
And as much of human frailty
As will make both ends just meet;
A brookletful of passion
And a riverful of love,
The wisdom of a serpent
And the meekness of a dove;
Take a good big chunk of thoughtfulness
The same amount of care,
And as large a sense of humour
As the Doctor says you dare;
A tiny bit of cussedness
A good deal more of spice,
And just enough of goodness
So as not to be too nice;
Now mix these all together
For better or for worse;
Take a bucketful at bedtime
And you'll be a perfect nurse.

Sometimes a patient felt that he should be receiving 'more reasonable and humane treatment', as a budding flautist described his problems in a letter to the *Gifford Journal*. One day, having to stay in bed, he decided that this was a good opportunity to practise the flute, which he was trying to learn. He obtained the agreement of the only other occupant of the ward and began to practise. After five minutes, he noticed someone standing by the door sniffing and looking around anxiously. When she caught his eye, she said: 'What an awful escape of gas there is somewhere'. He continues:

> This was not very encouraging but nothing daunted, I carried on. Some few minutes later, in came a Sister who calmly asked me if I wanted my pipe and tobacco pouch. After that I went to work very quietly thinking to disturb no one but it was useless. Within a minute or two in came a Nurse with two bananas which she presented to me with Matron's compliments, and said, would I have these instead of the flute?

Our frustrated flautist put away his instrument and in future resorted to practising in any odd corner of the grounds, although even then he was chased away because 'the male nurse cannot sleep'. He also complains about 'the unpleasant habit people have of dropping pennies near the budding musician'; this, in itself, was not too bad, but 'to pick them up again and walk away is the last word in impudence'!

Sometimes there were practical problems which are faced by any hospital patient, as experienced when someone working in the hospital shared a bedroom with two colleagues. 'He snored heavily—in all keys, compass unlimited and variations ad lib.' The other two tried to sleep but in vain. 'Presently a crescendo of snores passing through three octaves ended in a climax startling in its intensity.' This woke up even the sleeper himself who startled his companions by exclaiming: 'If you fellows don't give up snoring I shall throw something at you. You've woke me up!' Some problems never change and the snores still echo around the wards today.

But we will now leave the wards themselves to see the facilities which were available in other parts of the hospital.

CHAPTER 5

◆

AWAY FROM THE WARDS

If the emphasis of Gifford House was on the continuing care for the disabled soldier, it was natural that a considerable amount of attention should be paid to therapeutic activities away from the wards. As today, everyone who is able to be up and about is encouraged to take part in activities which not only help any process of rehabilitation, but also serve to pass the time constructively, meaningfully and pleasantly. This was perhaps one of the most important understandings to be gained through having to care for young, injured soldiers whose lives, damaged by war, were now having to be directed along paths which beforehand might have seemed alien. On the one hand there was the process of having to readjust to a sedentary way of life, on the other an acceptance of the loss of function of limb or body. Whatever the particular disability, the emphasis was on the whole man and this meant all the legitimate needs which he faced during his time under the care of the hospital home. Not that discharge was ever guaranteed or denied in advance; rather, each patient was recognised as having his own individual needs and these were met as far as practicable.

So let us now look at those activities which were provided for anyone who could use them to their advantage, which may previously have been hobbies or pastimes but which now took on a greater significance and interest.

Alterations were put in hand to adapt the building for internal activities. The concert room in the basement was converted into a Day Room; a small billiard table was installed and it was in this room that many of the social activities were held, as we shall see. Access to the room was made easier by building a slope for the wheelchairs. The massage rooms were turned into workshops. Finance for these workshops came from the Ministry of Pensions which had purchased the plant and two electric lathes from Queen Mary's Hospital, Roehampton. An instructor was appointed to see that the men could receive training in many forms of handicraft. The Ministry would provide the materials required during training but afterwards the men had to buy it for themselves, and received the money realised on the sale of the articles they had made. The billiard room was itself converted to house the displaced massage room and in the evenings it could be used by the orchestra for practice sessions. This delighted the musicians, for the room was noted for its acoustic qualities. The announcement of these plans by Mrs. Hay resulted in the patients raising three resounding cheers for her (something which reflects how methods of appreciation have changed over the years).

Much of the activity centred around the workshops. By the end of 1920, apparatus for woodwork had been installed and this was the major activity for the immediate future. The workroom was fitted with shelves to a degree of professionalism which went so far as to suggest that 'a professional carpenter could not have done better'. This did not mean that the amateur attempts were always completely successful; one of the men, wishing to sharpen a lead pencil and scorning the use of a pen-knife in favour of a wood chisel, found himself the unhappy recipient of bandages which were to curtail his activities for sometime, having ignored the golden rule (left hand always behind the cutting edge). A trained electrician installed the necessary electric batteries (an indication of the difference in facilities in those days) and, having done so, offered his services as

24   *The Workshop*

'O.C. glue-pot'. (This brings back memories of the interminable time it could take to bring some types of glue to a working consistency and also of the obnoxious smells which some brands emitted; no luxury of such modern products as epoxy resins and super-glue.)

There seems to have been a large number of carpenters, judging by the amount of sawdust and shavings which were generated. Several new cages were made for the aviary though there were some problems with the mixing of the paint; after three coats had been applied, there was still no change in the colour of the wood! One patient spent his time, apparently very successfully, constructing a fowl-house for the hospital poultry. Pigeon lofts also became part of the production line and were indeed in some demand from the very popular pigeon fanciers, as we shall shortly see. The installation of lathes, grindstones and jig-saws increased the potential production lines. Broken furniture was mended and a good deal of French polishing undertaken. As experience was gained and skills were refined, so toy-making became a new venture, including railway engines, scooters and black cat mascots, together with medicine chests and stools.

Alongside the carpentry was installed a successful boot-repairing section. Apparently, the repairers were always busy and their work increasing, a sure sign of their standards of excellence. One such repairer was quoted as saying that he always enjoyed his evenings better after a hard day's work and this was apparently evident as the evenings wore on! There must have been a considerable saving through this work as well as the satisfaction of work which was both necessary and appreciated. (What would they have done in a world of 'trainers' and non-repairable footwear?)

The basket-making industry was also highly successful. The patients were taught by a Miss Palmer who had worked at the King George Hospital and who was happy to continue her work at Gifford House. She had been encouraged in the first place by Mrs. Hay, and her tuition resulted in some very creditable fine cane and raffia work. The basket makers found themselves under great pressure as each Christmas approached and this was followed by the inevitable slump in demand in the following month or so.

By the beginning of 1922, mat and rug making were being added to the range of activities. At this time, a specific gift was being prepared—a wedding gift for H.R.H. Princess Mary. This took the form of a tapestry stool and the men who had done the work were chosen to form the deputation to Buckingham Palace on 13 February accompanied by Mrs. Hay. The tapestry had been woven by Pensioner J. Marshall, the carpentry done by Pensioners Weldin and Holl, the French polishing by Pensioner G. Buck, the upholstering by Pensioners Archer and Green and the illuminated address by Pensioner R. S. Brunning. These men were delighted with their visit and by the way in which the Princess spoke with each of them individually. A press account of the event, labelled rather patronisingly 'Crippled Soldiers' Offering', records that one group of patients came by wheelchair, the other was able to walk to the Palace. The Princess talked 'sympathetically to each of her visitors' and thanked them for their gift in these words:

> I am deeply touched by the kindly thought of the patients of the Queen Alexandra Hospital Home for Disabled Soldiers in coming here this morning to present me with this beautiful stool and address. It gives me the greatest pleasure to receive these gifts, and it is especially interesting to know that the stool has been made and the address illuminated by the patients themselves. I thank the donors with all my heart.

By mid-1922 the rug-making department was coming under the eye of the patients and in particular of one S. Oliver, who was inspired to write this account as he suffered from a severe case of tongue in cheek. Entitled 'A Peep into the Rug-making factory', he described how the process worked:

> First the Junior Partner is sent into the country to buy some sheep at as low a price as possible, he interviews Farmer Jenkins, inspects the sheep from which he selects the most woolly ones, these are sent carriage paid, to the firm's depot where they are placed in pens in the open and marked first, second and third grade wool.
>
> The next man to handle the sheep is the dipper or dyer, who is given a list of colours required, he then dyes a number of sheep according to the amount of wool required of each colour, after the sheep have been in the dying vats till they attain the required shade, they are taken in the open to dry. Next the barber comes forward and cuts off the wool, this is then taken into another department and made up into balls and skeins, and the surplus into bales for stock.
>
> There are seven workers in the factory, each having his own special job as Cutters, Threaders, Weavers, Colour schemers and various other schemers. Most of the work is done by hand and it is a wonderful sight to watch the nimble fingers travel along in this beautiful work of art. Some of the rugs turned out are of such a large size that they take two months to make.
>
> All orders will receive prompt attention and complete satisfaction will be given, please address all orders to Messrs Levi & Co, Ward 4. You are invited to inspect the show rooms at any time.

(The writer goes on to note that in Army parlance he would be termed '51.A.R.'!)

The primary purpose of the workshop was therapeutic but the products became helpful in raising cash for the workshop and so we find that, as today, articles made by the patients were put on sale both at the summer fetes and Christmas fairs. For example, two exhibitions and sales of work were held in December 1921. The first was held at the premises of a Mr. T. Button in London Road, Kingston on two days. Having lent his shop for the purpose, a splendid array of articles was set out—hand-painted lamp shades, powder-bowls and calendars, various wooden toys, baskets, gold and silver wire beads, rugs, mats, light articles of furniture, French-polished trays and beadwork butterflies. Aided by a window display, and Pensioner Anderson who assisted Mr. Button, the highly satisfying sum of £19 was realised. The unsold items were then exhibited, with others, at a sale in Worple Road, Wimbledon on premises kindly lent by the St George's Sunday School at the request of Mr. Whitehead (whom we shall meet shortly). This gentleman apparently threw himself wholeheartedly into this event and his great enthusiasm for the cause helped towards achieving a profit of over £55. These two supporters of Gifford House were clearly playing an important role and one dares to suppose that Lady Ripon would have thoroughly approved of their efforts. Enthusiastic supporters continue to contribute today to the welfare of the Hospital Home, thus carrying on the tradition which Lady Ripon began.

In the following summer the workshops were again busy preparing for the Garden Fete and Exhibition. This time we find additional articles—fern stands, medicine cabinets, book racks, tea-pot stands, painted powder bowls, lamp shades and water-colour paintings and drawings. One very popular line was the woodcuts produced by one J. M. Marshall. Carved on boxwood, they depicted country scenes and signed, hand-painted versions were eagerly snapped up for decorations for small rooms. The following December, it was 'on the road again', this time to an exhibition and sale at the premises of Mr. H. Offer, builder, in Victoria Road, near Surbiton Station.

It might seem, in comparison with today's sale of goods, that those of former years produced a bigger variety of articles. There is, however, one significant difference; the average age of patients was then very much lower, patients having come direct from active service in their teens and early twenties, and manual dexterity was more common than for many today.

A reminder of the youthfulness of the patients is that some instrumentalists began to get together and to enjoy music. For the first few weeks after the opening of Gifford House, this was limited to what was described as 'a somewhat crude Jazz Band'. Crude or not musically, it was an instant hit, probably because the players achieved a maximum amount of pleasure and noise in spite of having only a minimum knowledge of the theory of music, as one critic of the day suggested. 'One can play a drum or a cymbal in a jazz band without knowing the difference between a crescendo and a three bars rest'. Some of the men were taking up the study of music and investigating the mysteries of various instruments. From those explorations it was hoped that an orchestra might be formed to rival the jazz band in popularity. Early in 1920 we find that, at the party given in honour of the retiring Matron, the most popular feature was indeed the Jazz Band which appeared again at the Bazaar in aid of the hospital and according to the *Wandsworth Boro News* the 'musical ability of the performers was second only to the vim with which they played their instruments'. And as one patient wrote to the *Journal* under a pseudonym: 'Heard the band practising today as they unkindly left the doors open. Was not surprised from the noise I heard that even the conductor was overcome and had to retire for an interval of rest and quiet before resuming his duties'.

One of the very popular activities which quickly became established was that of the Pigeon Club. Its formation was made easier by the offer of Mr. Charrington, the owner of Gifford House, to loan the excellent lofts in the grounds near the house. They were especially suitable for the patients, being on ground level and easily accessible to anyone in a wheelchair.

The initial stock consisted of about 50 fine birds, 15 pairs of which were sent by Lt. W. D. Osman, O.C. Pigeon Service, Royal Air Force (which may perhaps bring a smile to those who have known the RAF in more technically advanced times or those who have not had the privilege of serving in the light blue and feel that pigeons are perhaps still in service!). Ten other pairs were lent by benefactors in Putney, Willenhall, Staffordshire and Coventry. Some of the staff also belonged to the club which was financed by a weekly subscription of 1s. It was linked to the nearest Flying Club at Fulham.

Their first season of flying turned out to be more rewarding than might have been expected. Most of the birds were young and therefore not expected to win many honours, especially as they

25 *Members of the Pigeon Club*

were being flown against experienced fanciers. However, in the six races, the Club obtained a fourth, a fifth and a seventh as well as winning the 10s. prize for novices. This stimulated several local clubs to give their encouragement and offer a prize of £8 to be competed for by the Gifford House club. Club members were arranged in pairs, each drawing a bird before the race, the results being reckoned on average velocity. The first prize went to Sgt. Shepherd and R. Perkins; the former also won a further special prize of 5s. and Sister Palmer and her friends contributed a further 30s. prize. Earlier in the season, Sgt. Shepherd had offered to the Fulham Club a prize of £2 to be competed for by ex-servicemen who had not won a first, second or third in club races. By a strange coincidence, the prize was won by the Gifford House club! The prize was passed on to the next competitors.

The competitors put much store into the way in which the birds had been trapped and clocked in. Messrs Tilney, Mann and Thompson received special thanks for their work and for taking the birds to the marking station before each race. Mr. York, a member of the staff, was thanked for regularly giving up his Saturday evenings to take the clock to the club house and to wait to hear the results of the races. The question of winter quartering then began to exercise their minds, for it was hoped that in their next season the birds would be flown on cross-Channel races. Their hopes were reasonably fulfilled. By the end of the 1921 season, the club had made the best average in the Fulham Club. Their best win was from Marennes when their bird covered a distance of 391¼ miles with a velocity of 811 yards per minute. In a race with the Barnes and Mortlake Club they lost by the narrow margin of only 47 yards. For the cognoscenti, their first winner was a Red Chequer Cock bred from a Red Pied Hen and a Blue Cock. The birds from the Royal Air Force had a splendid season as did some of the younger birds, the best of which recorded a velocity of 1689 yards per minute in its best race. Not surprisingly, fanciers from local clubs became interested and were very welcome visitors to the new enthusiasts.

The club organised a show on 14 January 1922 thanks to the support of the South Western Federation. There were 250 birds in the show. The most famous was 'Crisp V.C.' a bird which had carried a message and saved one of His Majesty's warships, and another bird which had saved a platoon in Gallipoli. The 'best bird' prize was awarded to Gifford's 'Lady Rome'. The prize distribution on 28 January by Sir Arthur Stanley was also the occasion for the presentation of an auto-attachment for the new Argson chair procured for them by Mrs. Hay; it was felt that this motor chair would be a great advantage to the bird fanciers in the coming season. (We shall hear more of the adventures enjoyed in these chairs.) Mrs. Hay had presented a cup for the highest points awarded to three nominated birds and the club members made a thoughtful gesture in presenting to the Matron a silver mounted oak biscuit barrel which they had won as a prize in one of their races.

The news of the 1922 season was less comforting. In races to Lymington and Bournemouth the birds did not make much of an impression and one of them returned with its ring cut off, thus eliminating it from any further competitive activity. And on a sadder note one of the club's oldest members, Mr. A. Shepherd, had 'now gone home and taken a few birds with him and a loft was made in the workshops in his memory'.

The performance of the birds in the next two years fell short of expectations and this had a slightly depressing effect on the members. The *Punch* cartoonist, Mr. Bert Thomas, did try to cheer up the club by drawing for them a cartoon entitled 'The Pouting Profiteer' which was drawn on the assumption that they had won all the available prizes. The disappointments were those often faced by fanciers, such as the young bird which would have won its race had it not decided to remain on the roof of the loft for over half an hour before it consented to enter the trap!

There was a Canary Club which had been stocked and supplied by the practical help of Mrs. Hay. The autumn of the year was regarded to be the most difficult, being the moulting season; the older birds required a good deal of attention not least in their diet. But the new cages were extremely satisfactory and in time a fair number of young birds were reared. Indeed, the number of birds increased greatly, both young songsters and Yorkshires, and were sold when they were surplus to need.

A more predictable activity was that of the Camera Club. The House Committee had ensured that an excellent Dark Room was set up and much of the necessary apparatus was loaned by Mr. J. Parker Fowler, the Hon. Sec. of the club. He also gave weekly lectures dealing with all branches of photography from the most elementary processes to the making of lantern slides and enlargements. The classes were held on Monday afternoons and were recommended as being a way in which to achieve quick progress in photographic competency.

Modern-day enthusiasts may be interested to read about one of his typical lectures. On one occasion, he spoke about the effect of light and colour. Of the colours of which white is made up, the blues have most affect on the plate, the reds have least, while the greens and yellows come somewhere in between. Several ways had been introduced to overcome this difficulty, such as the orthochromatic plate, the self-screen plate and the panchromatic plate, each of which became more efficient when used with a suitable light filter. He went on to explain how, by taking further advantage of the various screens at the photographer's disposal, it was possible to emphasise all objects of a given colour which the subject contained by cutting off, to a certain extent, the other colours. Similarly, it was possible to eliminate all parts of the subject of a given colour by using a screen which allows only the other colours to pass through. The club's first exhibition was held on 1 March 1920 with a prize of 5s. being awarded for the best print.

An altogether more physical event took place in the summer of 1920, namely the first croquet tournament. The vagaries of the English weather do not seem to have changed, for it is recorded that the tournament was held in the only real spell of summer weather of the whole year. The indomitable Sgt. Shepherd was the driving force behind the event, energetically backed up by the Matron and staff. The latter exhibited the kind of reaction that might have been expected, making such comments as: 'Never played in my life', 'Haven't touched a mallet for years', but such pleas fell on deaf ears as the canvassers guaranteed to teach them the basic techniques and wheedled out of

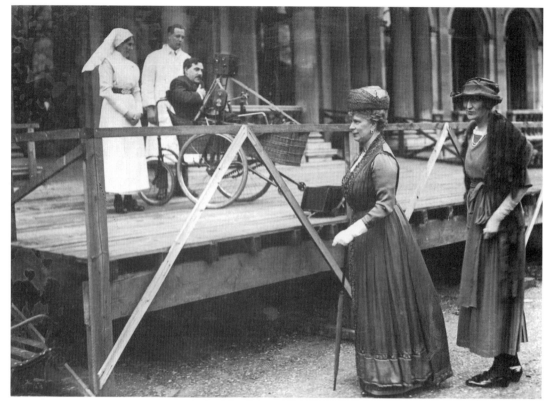

26   *Queen Mary with Lady Juliet; an enthusiastic member of the photographic club on the ramp.*

them the entry fee of one shilling. Away in a quiet corner of the grounds, the weak ones were coached and given a degree of confidence which finally got them to the tournament itself.

Matron's skill (her very accurate strokes were commented upon) saw her and her partner win through their first round match but Sister Palmer was handicapped by her 'rookie' partner and was defeated. Nurse Murrell played outstandingly in her round but to no avail. Nurse Smyth and Sister Bush had better fortune, though one of their opposing pair, both patients, was overheard to make a protest to the effect that there was no umpire; a deep voice from the occupant of a chair just behind him reassured him that all was well. A losing pair of nurses was thought to have suffered from the efforts of an orchestra which happened to be practising close by! One patient, who had never previously played, performed acrobatic feats and was a source of considerable amusement to the onlookers. The second round and the semi-finals proceeded in a similar manner and the final, played on another day, resulted in a seven-hoop win for Nurse Musgrave and Miss Crispin (who later went on to win the tennis final with Nurse Dodder-Smyth).

Matron carried out the prizegiving and did so by freely giving sound advice to the winners in a way which greatly amused the crowd but apparently left the winners in a state of blushing confusion. Thanks were also given to Buck, the groundsman and the whole event seems to have been conducted enthusiastically and in high spirits.

In the *Gifford Journal* of October 1920, we read about the work which Mrs. Hay had been doing in regard to what was termed 'Off Duty' time. She called a meeting of all the patients to tell them about arrangements which had been made 'for the more interesting and profitable ways' of spending such time. As the classes at Roehampton had now ceased and winter was approaching, the men would have to spend more time indoors. It is difficult not to come to the conclusion that her talk developed into something of a lecture, for the *Journal* reports that she gave 'some sound advice on the subject of certain pastimes which, carried on to too great an extent only resulted in lowering the tone of the hospital'. She then went on to explain in detail a scheme of banking which she herself had planned and arranged, and 'which the men agreed unanimously was to everyone's advantage to use'.

The Day Room was opened on 1 November 1920 and was celebrated by a concert given by a Mr. Hayden and his party, 'ably assisted by his lady friends', and this resulted in an enjoyable time. Three days later there was a conjuring display where apparently even the sharpest card players among the patients were completely mystified. Six days later there was a cinema show given by Capt. Cottle from the Church Army.

Mrs. Hay next tackled the Christmas festivities. She announced that the entertainments would be held early in the week of Christmas Day so that those patients who qualified for a free railway warrant in order to travel home might still enjoy the festivities. These began with a concert entirely arranged by the patients, and the orchestra took a leading part in it under the direction of Pensioner Dawson. Sgt. Shepherd organised a tournament of indoor games. Two days later, the Tea Party was held with a large Christmas tree in the Hall with presents for both patients and staff. Patients who were unable to go home were encouraged to invite a relation or friend to spend Christmas at the hospital.

The Day Room became the centre for social activities. Sometimes the staff themselves were not averse to doing some entertaining; at the time of Matron Harte's departure the songs by Sister Brown and Nurse Rowden were greatly appreciated and they were joined by two of the patients, 'Jock' Taylor and Sgt. Shepherd (who seems to have been a driving force in many activities).

The patients and staff at Gifford House have always valued the interest which members of the Royal family have shown over the years. King George V and Queen Mary paid an informal visit on 30 March 1920. They made a detailed inspection of the Home and spoke to many of the 70 patients. They saw men engaged in cabinet-making, speaking with approval of the quality of the work. In one of the workshops, the Queen recognised Albert Butler who had sold lacquer work articles to her at Central Hall, Westminster. They chatted with those who were confined to their beds as well as those attending to the chickens, the pigeons and the canaries. They also encountered Winifred the goat who was renowned for following the patients about in their invalid chairs. The King was heard to comment: 'Goats have a wonderful appetite, and will eat almost anything'. As if to give point to this remark, Winifred immediately picked up and swallowed a packet of cigarettes which a member of the party had dropped. Then she started to eat the tassel of the scarf worn by Mrs. Hay and next turned her attention to the dress of a lady-in-waiting, whereupon she was 'confined to barracks' until the Royal party had left.

As our history unfolds we shall see that the interest of the Royal family continued, much to the delight of everyone, as this was a sure sign of the importance which they attached to the work of the hospital.

Many visitors were pleased to come to Gifford House, often at the invitation of a governor or Patron with whom they were connected. Thus famous names such as George Robey, Percy Kahn and Miss Lilian Hoare appeared (as they had at the King George Hospital). But less prestigious guests also delighted the patients. A visit by a group of girls from Putney High School was a cause of considerable pleasure; we are told that they made 'a brave show in their fancy dress' treating the patients to some 'amusing games' and, after tea, 'to a really remarkable concert'.

One of the most popular visiting groups were the girls from the Regent Telephone Company who were regular visitors during the Roehampton years. Their concerts were always well attended; indeed, on one occasion when their visit clashed with a football match, a large number of the patients preferred to enjoy their entertainment, consisting of an excellent tea and concert.

27 *King George V inspects the chickens; Lady Juliet Duff is on his right, Mrs. Hay looks on and a group of nurses watches from the ramp.*

One patient was inspired to write from time to time a saga of 'The Giffites' and his piece about these girls is positively lyrical:

> Now there came to the House of Giff from a land afar off, even that country which is called the Land of Wires, certain fair damsels. And these did sing to the men of Giff, and make them merry and did bring them cakes from the Land of Wires. Now there were some men of the House of Giff who did lose their hearts unto the damsels from the Land of Wires, and strange were the things they did. And there was one Trupa of whom it was said that his hair and his eyes had found favour with the damsels. So he strayed not from the House of Giff but did appear before the damsels with his hair well placed—and the half of it was towards one side and the other half that was towards the other side and the place between, that was straight as the rod with which men draw a line.

The rapport flourished and the men invited 50 of the girls to a concert at Gifford House on 18 February 1922. One of the girls, writing about the event, describes how their 'highest imaginings were more than realised; for the whole affair, from the eggs and tomatoes to "God Save the King" was a splendid success'.

The invitation was to tea and a concert. 'Imagine', says this young lady, 'the responsibility of entertaining fifty laughing, chattering, irresponsible members of the feminine species! Still, these particular warriors at Gifford House have had much practice and experience—we inflict ourselves upon them periodically—and they make an excellent job of it'.

Excellent indeed, for after a sumptuous tea everyone moved to the ballroom, programmes for the concert were handed out, the curtains were drawn back and the entertainment began. The wonderful costumes had a particular effect on the guests, who marvelled at the blends of colours, the suits fashioned by nimble fingers and the electric lights 'frivolous in their gay streamers of yellow, orange and black'. The orchestra seems to have excelled itself and the mellow voices of the singers won over the hearts of their guests. The hit of the show was 'Margie' who 'came on in all his—I mean "her"—grace and beauty and her ravishing attire'. Apparently, on the following Monday morning, all the subscribers on the Regent Exchange remarked upon the 'Sweetness and Angelic Patience' of their telephonists!

These may have been the most popular visitors but the Entertainments Committee, chaired by Matron, arranged many events. Local visitors continued to stream in—dramatic and concert societies, individual performers and school children, one such group from the Warple Road school amazing many by their splendid rendering of *HMS Pinafore*. Matron's experiences at the Bolingbroke were clearly yielding fruit, not least in the principle of running 'home-made' amusements; a levy of one shilling per head throughout the hospital seems to have amply justified the outlay. But there was much to occupy the men in activities outside the house and grounds.

One of the most appreciated activities for any patient was the opportunity to leave the building and the grounds, and to get out into the 'world' for the stimulation of fresh air, sounds and faces. That is still a feature of the life of Gifford House today and the invitations to outside events are always a welcome feature of daily life. The tradition began at Roehampton.

One of the earliest records mentions that the Duchess of Wellington lent her box at the Royal Albert Hall and this enabled a group of patients to hear a performance of *Messiah* given by the Royal Choral Society at Christmas 1919 (perhaps a relief from the rudimentary noises issuing from the practice room of the Giffites' orchestra!). Not that the form of transport on such occasions always seems to have been the most comfortable: a photograph from the *Daily Graphic* shows patients arriving for the Victory Circus and Allied Fair in a large Harrods van showing the inscription 'Estimates Free'! They were carefully 'unloaded' down a ramp under the watchful eye of a policeman.

One of the most active benefactors was a Mr. E.W. Whitehead and a group of his friends from the Order of Freemasons. His involvement began in January 1921 when he arrived at Gifford House with a fleet of cars and took some of the patients to see an afternoon performance of *Cinderella* at the Wimbledon Theatre. After the show, they were whisked away to the *Wimbledon Hill Hotel* for an excellent dinner. Mr. Whitehead's friends and helpers ensured that they were comfortable and had a happy time. In expressing the wish that he would be hoping to give the patients further entertainments, it appears from their reaction that they had already given him high marks for the party which they had just enjoyed.

In January 1923 about 20 patients, together with over 200 from various hospitals around the Surrey and Middlesex borders, were the guests of the Freemasons of Surbiton and District at their hall in Surbiton, to a high tea and entertainment. The comment was made that Mr. Whitehead 'and his brethren of the Craft' never did things by half, and that was again true on that occasion. In fact, the format was repeated only a fortnight later, this time at Wimbledon. The guests, from local hospitals, numbered over 350. Again there was an excellent spread and a concert; this included 'the drolleries of Mr. F. Hook and Mr. Hastings, the clever banjo solos of Miss Courtenay, and the delightful singing of Miss Muriel Whitehead and Mr. Vincent'. The band of the East Surrey Regiment provided some excellent musical selections.

Mr. Whitehead was also closely involved with an outing to the Derby. There were two charabancs, which Mrs. Hay provided, enabling about 50 patients to enjoy the outing—except, that is, for those who expected more from the bookies; one patient wrote that his bookie 'remembered a pressing appointment just as our favourite horse got home'. This trip came to be one of the most popular of the year. For the 1922 meeting, Mr. Whitehead obtained good viewing positions for

28   *'Giffites' at Wimbledon Theatre, 1922*

them near the starting post. Although the 46 Giffites had set out with the intention of backing a winner and avoiding being 'welched', it is reported that they spent their return journey in a rather contemplative manner. Such postures can still be witnessed in Gifford House today!

Other outings provided a sting of another kind. Nearby Richmond Park was a natural place for expeditions in groups or singly, especially for those with motorised chairs (of which more later). Unfortunately, however delightful the park may have appeared, it was more than adequately populated by flies. One patient who had experienced this problem, had this laconic advice:

> If you find the flies with which the place is swarming continually interrupt that tale you are telling to your interested audience (say of one) and you find yourself short of cigarettes, a simple method of attack is to pack bracken leaves in the upper part of your cycle lamp and light the wick. The smoke will have the desired effect, while placing the lamp in a conspicuous position (should the tale not prove interesting) a diversion can be created by studying the pictures in the burning bracken.

Richmond Park was to be the scene of many an outing for a variety of purposes, individually or accompanied, at different hours of the day and evening; anonymous comments in the *Gifford Journal* avoid mentioning any names but the catch-phrases used will have been clearly identifiable by observer and observed alike.

Charabancs were put to regular use. On 6 July 1921, a party of staff and patients went to Sunningdale (some patients went in an ambulance) where they were entertained to tea by Sir Reginald and Lady Cox. Sir Reginald was a senior partner of the bankers, Cox & Co., and played an important part in advising the Governors on financial matters. After the tea, the whole party took a steamer down the river to Hampton Church, the Giffites leaving their hosts 'with cheers of approbation', and arriving back at 9.30pm.

Less than two weeks later, another charabanc outing took a party to Leatherhead. The following month, two-thirds of the patients were taken by charabanc and car to Brighton for the day. They made an early start and some were able to enjoy the beach for four hours; it is not difficult to imagine the pleasure this must have given.

Then there was the garden party in Surbiton in the grounds of the Masonic Hall organised by—Mr. Whitehead. It was on a 'lavish scale' which seems to have characterised the way in which he approached the events under his command. Patients from other hospitals were there; the event was blessed with brilliant sunshine. Mr. Whitehead further endeared himself to the Giffites by asking their orchestra to perform during the afternoon—they seem to have gained in status and competence as time passed. But sadly the link with Mr. Whitehead came to an end with his death in January 1924. An obituary notice in the *Journal* ran as follows:

> It is with much genuine regret and sorrow that we report the death of our well known friend— Mr. E.W. Whitehead. His unfailing kindness and personal interest for the boys still in hospital, leaves us with many happy memories, but also leaves us with the more room for missing his cheerful personality. His name will ever hold a place in the annals of the Giffites.

And well it may, for by such benefactors are the lives of patients enriched.

Reference was made earlier to the motorised wheelchairs. Photographs of the time show what we regard today as the 'classic' chairs of the days of our grandparents—chairs constructed mainly of wicker, with baskets in front of the patient's feet or with long handles which enabled the patient to steer his course. Some were equipped with the additional rim on the wheels so that the

29   *The first river trip given by the 'Lest-We-Forget' Association*

patient could move under his own efforts, others were like 'chaises longues' enabling the patient to lie back and take life easy. But nothing compared with the invention of the engine which gave to chair and passenger a potential for mobility hitherto undreamed of.

These chairs were referred to as 'auto-wheelers'. They were, in fact, the Argson 'Standard' with a Villiers 147cc two-stroke engine with a two-speed and differential gear box and band brakes on the rear wheels. They made a tremendous noise. They had to be registered for use on public roads and were issued with registration numbers—such as XM 5194, XT 9453, YM 7381—which today would fetch a high price at auctions for those wanting cherished numbers on their cars. These chairs represented the 'new technology' of the day and became very much a 'craze' for those who were ready to explore their potential. But new technology meant teething problems, and these chairs were notoriously unreliable. The hours which had to be spent investigating and exploring the internal workings would 'turn an ardent jig-saw expert green with envy'. After having spent the best part of a day locating and correcting some small defect somewhere in the internal regions of the engine, it was not at all unusual to find, on starting the engine (or trying to) that 'you have got the thingummyjig just where the what-do-you-call-it should have been, and the oojah-bob too tight up against the fakalorum'. One newcomer to Gifford House spotted a man out of his chair sitting on the grass with parts of his machine scattered around him. His innocent question evoked a cynical and some what terse response, and he decided to take the matter no further! He was subsequently advised: 'Never approach a man on the subject of auto-wheels if you see him with his machine in pieces. Always go to the man whose engine is running well. You will always find someone. I have known times when there have been as many as two or three engines all running perfectly'.

Often the problem was merely that of overheating (the air-cooled engine was at the back). One patient, experiencing (as he thought) this phenomenon out on the road, stopped for the engine to cool down. A passing motorcyclist stopped to ask if there was any engine trouble, and if he could help. He was thanked for his interest but as soon as the engine cooled down the patient would be able to re-start. The motorcyclist proceeded on his way. Then at last the engine felt cool, the starting mechanism was engaged—and nothing happened. The Good Samaritan had disappeared over the horizon …

These chairs were also known to spill oil on the wards, and the linen staff complained about oil marks on shirt cuffs. The chairs did have something of a tempestuous life; they were used in croquet matches—the sudden changes of gear and application of brakes, the violent changes of direction and manoeuvres put a heavy strain on the machines. So, too, did the ramp which enabled the chair-bound to reach the lawns from the building; whilst the descent gave no problems, there was always a debate as to whether the ascent should be made gently in bottom gear or by an attack at maximum speed.

One of the best examples of the merits of these machines is shown in the trip taken by three patients to Eastbourne. At 5.50am on 12 July 1923, these three left Gifford House equipped with petrol, oil, tools, spares and sandwiches. Through Wimbledon, Mitcham and thence to Croydon where the roads were found to be atrocious, and on to Purley and Riddlesdown where the tyre of one of the chairs collapsed. The repair took only 15 minutes and the party moved on to Godstone, East Grinstead and Forest Row. About noon, the engine of another chair showed symptoms of breathlessness and was cured by an injection of paraffin. The drivers stopped at a pub where the host was discovered to be a former patient of the King George Hospital. After a chat, two quarts of petrol and a drink the journey continued via Hailsham and Polegate.

One of the drivers had journeyed without a hat and was forced to halt and take shelter under a shop window-blind. Opposite the shop, two young ladies waved from the window of their home, inviting him to refreshments with a wash and brush up, and they also gave him a straw hat.

When the intrepid travellers arrived at Eastbourne at the holiday home which was to provide hospitality for many patients over the years, they discovered to their chagrin that a fellow patient travelling from Gifford House by train had arrived just before them.

On their return journey, all went uneventfully until they reached Uckfield where a Ford 'tin lizzie' carrying mattresses and pillows burst its petrol tank and caught fire. (It was suggested that this was a mark of surprise by that vehicle at seeing the chairs running so impressively!) The fire brigade were summoned by the police blowing their whistles; the 'brigade' turned out to consist of two farm labourers working in a field nearby, who dived into a cottage, one having donned a helmet, the other a pair of top boots. They produced a manual fire engine which threw up a jet of water about three feet high from a tangled hose. By this time, the Ford was burnt out.

The smouldering ruins were left behind; over Ashdown Forest to take on petrol at East Grinstead and later at Whyteleafe. The straw-hatted patient found difficulty in starting his engine and traversed about a quarter of a mile by being pulled when it was pointed out that he might do better if he actually turned on the petrol! The happy trio reached Gifford House at 10.15pm very tired, painfully sunburnt and 'not quite so tidy as they had started out'.

In spite of the difficulties which inevitably arose with these machines, the patients were enormously grateful to Sir Arthur Stanley through whose generosity they were supplied by the British Red Cross Society. Indeed, the annual report of that society for the year ending 31 March 1923 states that 58 such machines were provided to several establishments on the recommendation of the Ministry of Pensions. They had proved very helpful to those whose only means of getting about was by hand-propulsion of their tricycles. Whilst today's equivalent machines do give some mechanical and electrical problems, contemplation of the earliest chairs does cause one to reflect on the significant technological advances made over 70 years; but would any patients today ever contemplate a day trip to Eastbourne?

CHAPTER 6

◆

BUSINESS STRATEGY

The responsibility for the overall welfare of Gifford House and of ensuring that it met its aims, rested with the Main Committee. Its Chairman was Colonel J.F. Badeley and the members were:

> Adeline, Duchess of Bedford
> Lady Juliet Duff (Lady Ripon's daughter)
> Lady Herbert
> Mrs. Algernon Hay
> Miss Dorothy Yorke
> Mr. W.F. Fladgate
> Sir William Goschen (Treasurer)
> Sir Arthur Stanley

Each of these members will have their own part to play as our story unfolds, but it will be helpful to draw a thumbnail sketch of the main players. Mrs. Algernon Hay had been a helper of Lady Ripon at the King George Hospital and she will figure strongly through the formative years of Gifford House; in fact, her sterling work covered a period of over 20 years and she is an example of long and dedicated service which has been given by employees and Governors. Mr. Fladgate had an extensive background in legal matters and was awarded the Medaille du Roi Albert, King of the Belgians, for services to Belgian lawyers during the war. Later he became chairman of the London Power Company and the Charing Cross Electricity Supply Company; he was also a director of Phoenix Assurance. Sir William Goschen was Deputy Chairman of the Finance Committee of the Red Cross and the Order of St John of Jerusalem. He was Chairman of the Sun Insurance Office and of Sun Life Assurance, and Commissioner of the Public Works Loan Board. Sir Arthur Stanley, who had an extensive philanthropic career, was Chairman of the Joint War Committee, Chairman of the Royal College of Nursing and Treasurer of St Thomas' Hospital; he was the brother of the 17th Earl of Derby. He had been permanently disabled by an attack of rheumatic fever in the

30 *Mrs. Verena Hay*

early 1890s which gave him frequent pain and confined him to a wheelchair in his later life; here was someone who could most readily understand the feelings and frustrations of the patients. Thus a considerable array of skills, qualities and contacts was gathered in this committee, which was to serve the cause of Gifford House with distinction.

31   *Ward 2, Roehampton*

The inaugural meeting was held on Monday 31 March 1919. The Chairman was Colonel Badeley, although the minutes record that he did not definitely undertake this role but would promise to do so if he could conscientiously with his other obligations. (In point of fact, he remained as Chairman until June 1920 and did not resign from the Committee until February 1924.) In addition to this committee, there was to be a Finance Committee and a House Committee. It is recorded that 'it was impossible in the present unformed state of things to define exactly what the business of the House Committee would entail' though suggestions included staffing levels, dismissal of staff etc., but that salaries would be the preserve of the Finance Committee. We concentrate now on the business of the main Committee, sometimes referred to as the 'General' or 'Executive' Committee in the Minutes; we shall use the latter title as being the most consistent.

The sum of £6,500 had been collected towards a memorial for Lady Ripon and it was agreed to hold this sum until some form of permanent memorial could be identified, although the sum of £80 15s. 6d. was authorised to cover the expenses incurred when looking at possible properties in Eastbourne and Brighton. This highlights one of the continuing concerns of the Governors—the house was only on loan from Mr. Charrington and the hospital would one day need to have a permanent home, a process which was to take nearly 14 years. The Treasurer was to be Sir Arthur Goschen, who announced his intention of banking at Cox's Bank. Then the discussion began to address itself to practical matters and specifically the appointment of a Registrar Secretary, who would live in 'and have some command over the men', and Matron could refer to him if in any difficulty with the men. 'It was agreed, with a few exceptions [Mrs. Hay?] that a woman could not fill this post satisfactorily.' The Chairman wanted to advertise quickly, suggesting a salary of £300 p.a., but this was thought to be too high and consultations would be held to assess the proper level of remuneration. What would he do when appointed? Make the returns, hold a small banking account so that Matron could apply for petty cash—that is all that we know about the job concept. Mrs. Hay had been looking at the staffing levels but expressed disappointment that she had not been able to discover any way of reducing the number of staff and this was also Matron's opinion. The latter was authorised to engage her staff at once although she must apply to Colonel Badeley for all Voluntary Aid Detachment (V.A.D.) help to avoid blocks. Good news for Matron, though; it was agreed that she should be paid from that time together with the two Sisters, the char-women, the stoker and the 'odd man' (presumably the 'job' was omitted from his title). Then Mrs. Hay took up the question of whether or not they should get permission for the hospital blues to have different shirts, ties etc., but Sir William pointed out that the men might be stopped for not being properly dressed according to Army rules. It was decided to research this further. Here is a reminder that Army discipline prevailed and it may seem quaint to some of today's patients that there should be a uniform to be worn and kept in the condition expected of an operational unit.

32   *The Hall used for dining and social occasions*

Mr. Charrington, the owner of Gifford House, had agreed the estimates for the alterations which were necessary but had specified that Messrs Adkins were to be instructed to carry out the work as he would accept no other firm.

Finally, Mrs. Hay reported that she had had a discussion with Colonel Webb about the number of patients who could be nursed, with the intention of ensuring that as large a number as possible were financed by the Ministry of Pensions. Colonel Sir Lisle Webb, who had served in the Royal Army Medical Corps in South Africa, was appointed Director General of Medical Services, Ministry of Pensions in 1919, which post he held until 1933, when he became secretary and treasurer of Queen Mary's Hospital, Roehampton; he was to prove a wise counsellor on many occasions over the years and had a thorough understanding of the needs of the patients and the Governors. He made it clear that he could not guarantee further cases other than the 39 already approved but he would not refuse any increase.

So ended the inaugural meeting of this influential committee, and we can see certain issues which would be regularly requiring the attention of the Governors:

1. Ensuring the maximum use of the beds available.
2. Achieving full financial support in terms of the capitation grant from Government.
3. Guaranteeing the permanence of the hospital in terms of its buildings.
4. Ensuring its financial health.

We shall now look at some of the issues which the Committee had to address; the pattern varies between those of high import and strategic considerations and comparative minutiae, as faced by many a committee in a like situation.

Staffing was one of the major concerns of the Committee. In these early days, their interest was in ensuring that the correct appointments were made, viz the experience necessary to work up the hospital from its starting point. The key appointment was felt to be that of Resident Medical Officer. This point was made strongly to the Committee by Colonel (later Sir E.) Farquhar Buzzard (Honorary Consulting Physician) and so an advertisement was placed in the *Lancet* offering a salary of £500. In due course, Dr. J. Todesco was appointed R.M.O.

Sir William Goschen was keen to ensure that a Secretary was appointed without further delay and Mrs. Hay hoped to find someone to fill the post temporarily until a permanent appointment could be made. This position was offered in May 1919 to Miss Kingsford, who had previously been secretary of Lady Litton's Hospital. A month later, Miss W. E. Bush was appointed as her assistant.

A rather startling reduction of the staff nurses from 18 to 12 was proposed by Colonel Badeley but the Matron was allowed to take a look at this suggestion with Mrs. Hay before any decision would be made (with a sigh of relief, no doubt!).

As we saw, the first Matron was Miss L. Pollock. One of her earliest recorded tasks was to draw up a set of Hospital Rules. These she presented to the Committee in June 1919 much to the satisfaction of the members, although they felt it necessary to specify a further rule forbidding patients or their friends to bring alcoholic drink into the Hospital. However, in November of that same year, the Committee were obliged to hold an emergency meeting to consider the resignation of Miss Pollock, and it was agreed that the post should be offered to Miss Harte, R.R.C. (Royal Red Cross).

Just over a month later, in December 1919, Miss Harte reported to the Committee that she had 'found a great deal of re-organisation necessary for the comfort of her Staff' and she was given permission to carry out any alterations which she thought desirable. What she discovered we do not know; perhaps it was that the staff conditions had not received the attention which they deserved simply because of the priority which had to be given to patients. Whatever the reason, it is still a characteristic of a change of incumbent that a new appointee will have different priorities. But Matron Harte did not have a long occupancy, and a one-line minute notes her resignation in January 1921. But a successor was quickly appointed—Miss L Fletcher, A.R.R.C., and this lady was to give loyal service to Gifford House for nearly four decades.

It appears that the ban on alcohol in the Matron's Rules did not entirely cater for all eventualities. For in January 1921, Mrs. Hay reported that certain patients had returned to the Hospital in an intoxicated condition. She had consulted Sir Lisle Webb regarding 'the infliction of a punishment'. An interesting choice of words! Sir Lisle proposed the following rule which was passed by the Committee.

'Any patient coming in intoxicated shall immediately be deprived of the use of his hand propelled chair for a fortnight the first time, and for one month the second time. If the patient prefers to leave the Hospital, he has the option of doing so, and on frequent repetition, he will, in any case be transferred'. At least, that was the original wording. An amendment was made to substitute for 'intoxicated' the phrase 'the worse for drink'! The Medical Superintendent asked that the resolution should not immediately be posted up but that he should hold it in readiness for the right moment. Then a further condition was imposed: 'It was also suggested that a man in an intoxicated(!) condition should not be allowed to go to his ward, but should be put in charge of an orderly and kept in a separate room for the night'. The R.M.O. was left with the responsibility for administering the rules at his discretion—whether the worse for drink or intoxicated, one assumes.

33   *Gifford House, facing the lake*

In June 1920 Mrs. Hay had to report to the Committee that the workshops at Queen Mary's Hospital, Roehampton were shortly to be shut down. Some patients had been benefiting from the opportunity to attend the workshops and she had therefore approached the Ministry of Pensions requesting that they consider the matter of the appointment of an instructor for the workshops at Gifford House. Her request was successful; two years later, however, the Ministry decided to reduce the salary of the instructor, Mr. Morgan, by £50 per annum. The Committee decided that in view of the invaluable assistance which Mr. Morgan was giving, and with the patients' various hobbies and occupations, the salary should be made good by the Compassionate Fund, another sign of the realistic and sympathetic decision-making which was a feature of the Committee and, indeed, the whole management. To judge by the success of the Open Days and sales of work on the many occasions over the years, this was an investment which yielded a consistently high return. Mr. Morgan was to remain a loyal employee for many years and not the least of his contributions was the sterling effort he put in during the move to Worthing.

The appointment and payment of a Chaplain for the Hospital seems to have had a rather chequered existence. The work of the Chaplain was initially carried out by one Brother Michael who was a member of a local Community to whom an annual payment of £50 was made, his travelling expenses being borne by the Compassionate Fund. However, in the summer of 1919 the Committee discussed Brother Michael's position, 'and after due consideration it was agreed that in view of the particular kind of patients at the Hospital, he should be requested to discontinue his services, although his intentions were of the best'. How were these intentions missing the mark? Did he have a level of churchmanship or a manner which the patients found unacceptable? We do not know. It is easy for us to feel a little sorry for Brother Michael, especially if his superior had given him the task and which had presumably been felt to be within his competency. Whatever the reason, it was arranged that a letter should be sent to the Duchess of Bedford letting her know about the decision and asking her to make the necessary arrangements to find a successor.

Her efforts were successful and three months later the Revd. R. Hibberd was appointed Chaplain 'at a stipend of £100 per annum' which Mrs. Hay had been able to fund 'from private sources locally'. However, in January 1920 Mr. Hibberd resigned. The reasons for this prompt parting are

34 *Christmas 1924*

not given but 'it was unanimously agreed that a letter be sent to him from the Committee, thanking him for his good work at the Hospital'. Once again Mrs. Hay found herself on the trail of a Chaplain and consulted a Canon Browne (perhaps the rural dean or someone with whom she was connected, we do not know) who promised to try to find a suitable candidate but asked that the Committee should do the same. In the meantime a Mr. Hanson acted as Chaplain for the Hospital and evidently to the satisfaction of the Committee, for two months later he was appointed Chaplain at the annual salary of £100 chargeable to the Hospital funds.

Mr. Hanson served as Chaplain for over four years. On his resignation in the summer of 1924, Mrs. Hay therefore again found herself in a search for a replacement. On this occasion she contacted the vicar of Putney to see whether he could take over the duties; the salary would be £100 per year (which was, in fact, a reduction from the £150 which had eventually been paid to Mr. Hanson—careful stewardship of money was still a continuing theme). The appointment was only made in January 1925 when the vicar agreed to undertake the Chaplain's duties himself. Many hospital management boards still face the same set of circumstances, including whether to appoint full-time (becoming a less favoured solution where funding is such a critical factor) or to identify a local clergyman whose duties allow some scope for extra-parochial activities (also a diminishing option).

The vicar of Putney went by the marvellously sounding name of E. Priestly Swain. He was inspired to write an open letter as follows:

My Dear Giffites,

I have just heard that you have a magazine and that the Editor is sending the next number to press immediately. So I write a short letter at once. As you know, the Committee have asked me to undertake the Chaplain's work, as Mr. Hanson has left, and Mr. Hosband, Mr. Cartridge and I are going to share the work between us. [Who were these gentlemen? More than likely curates of the parish of Putney although they may have been from another denomination.] We want to tell you that we hope you will regard us as your friends right away. We are anxious to do all we can to help and to be useful in any way that is possible. One great advantage for you in having three of us at work is that you will not so quickly get tired of our sermons, we hope. We promise not to make them very long. On the second Sunday in the month we hope to have a Celebration of Holy Communion after the usual morning service for the benefit of those of you who are communicants. The great event this month will be Christmas. People often forget that Christmas Day is a religious day. There are two things we ought to try and do. We should go to some service to give thanks to God for the wonderful gift of His Son to be born at Bethlehem for us. (There will be a service in your own chapel at 10.30am.) Secondly, we ought all to try and think of something we can do to make somebody else's Christmas happier. Wishing you all a happy Christmas.

No committee can hope to avoid the thorny question of expenses and this committee was no exception. Nurses' expenses were one such item. As early as July 1919, Colonel Badeley, Chairman, reported to the Committee that the Ministry of Pensions would not issue vouchers for the nurses' journeys. It was arranged, therefore, that a list should be compiled to show the travelling expenses incurred by nurses on taking up their duties at the hospital. That was in July; at the next meeting, in October, it was reported (by whom, we do not know) that the list would not be presented 'owing to the fact that there had been many changes in the staff, and it had not been found expedient to pay for the nurses' journeys'. Whether or not the granting of a bonus shortly afterwards to Sisters and nurses who had completed one year's service was a factor in the decision-making we cannot tell, but the problem obviously would not go away, for the decision was made in the following June that 'half of the Sisters' and nurses' travelling expenses be paid every six months after one year's service'. Perhaps this represents a compromise, perhaps it recognised the point which the Matron made quite forcibly, namely that she was finding it increasingly difficult to recruit nursing staff as other hospitals offered higher salaries.

If Parkinson's Law had been promulgated in those days, then everyone who had any dealings with the ticklish matter of the Gifford House car would have quoted that law 'ad infinitum'. In June 1919 it was decided that it was necessary to have a motor car for the Hospital. No doubt with an eye to the best buy, the Committee made application to the Demobilisation Committee for an ambulance chassis, upon which a convertible body could be fitted. This committee, as its name implies, had the responsibility of winding up the boards and committees which had been set up during the war as part of its necessary pursuance; these were now largely redundant, and in some respects the Demobilisation Committee had the nature of an Army Surplus agency. Upon application, however, it was discovered that the chassis had already been disposed of, but Sir William Goschen thought that it would be beneficial if application were to be made to that same committee for a landaulette. This seems to have been unsuccessful for, soon afterwards, Mrs. Hay is given the authority to write to a Mr. Sage, a 'Motor Contractor', to ask him to acquire a large landaulette body. This the worthy gentleman was able to do for the price of £90 and he was subsequently given an order to fit and paint it at a cost of a further £40. (One assumes that a chassis had been acquired from another source.) Simultaneously, efforts were to be made to recruit a chauffeur as soon as possible.

These decisions were made in January 1920 but by the end of May, at an emergency meeting of the Committee (to consider the resignation of the Resident Medical Officer), it was 'decided that steps should be taken to sell the car'. One would like to know the reasons behind this cryptic Minute! We can guess that the running costs were proving to be too high when considered against the benefits. Mrs. Hay was authorised to 'make arrangements for the hire of a car whenever she required one, chargeable to Hospital Funds'. It would seem unusual for the Committee to have given authority for a car just for the benefit of Mrs. Hay (though doubtless it would have recognised her indefatigable efforts on behalf of the hospital) or the vehicle could also have been available for the use of patients. Be that as it may, we conclude that the costs were thought to be excessive and the car was sold through an agency which, after deductions for commissions etc., realised the sum of £530.

For the financially curious reader who will ask whether a good return on this decision was achieved, the facts of the matter can be summed up thus. In the next two years, the cost of hiring cars totalled £540, and the average yearly cost for the next eight years was £176. Today the hospital owns no car but does have a substantial investment in coaches.

There was the need to set up a laundry facility so that as much work as possible could be done on the premises. Part of the stables were converted to meet this end. Similarly, the Committee wanted to identify a part of the building which could be converted into a mortuary and also for a chapel. The latter was completed by autumn 1919 with the exception of the lighting and heating which Mr. Charrington undertook to defray.

The question of staff accommodation became a real issue in 1920. Mrs. Hay was able to report that the Director General of Medical Services (Sir Lisle Webb) had arranged for the hospital to be affiliated to the Tooting Neurological Hospital, which would mean that cases from there would be sent to Gifford House. The Matron would consider the staffing implications, but also pressing was that of the increased accommodation for the staff which would result from this decision. Mrs. Hay pointed out that all the accommodation for friends and relations of the patients had already been monopolised for the use of the staff, as re-arranged by the Matron. (Does the word 'monopolised' suggest a frisson of frustration?) Enquiries would have to be made in the village to see if there was any scope there. Failing that, there would have to be a building programme, the expense being defrayed from the Savoy Chapel Fund, provided that their sanction was obtained. (The later formal link with the charity was to be one of the seminal events in the development of Gifford House in Worthing.) The response of the Royal Savoy Association was positive; they authorised the expenditure of £200 for the erection of a hut 'in order that the Hospital may still continue to accommodate patients' relations from time to time'. The Association also made a grant of £500 for providing patients with tools and necessaries for starting in business and with furniture for a home. This is a reminder of the absence of social support from the State which is perhaps today taken for granted. The money could also be used to transport patients to entertainments and for visits to their homes.

One of the most important activities of the Committee was to ensure that the finances were maintained on a healthy basis through the prompt receipt of grants for which the patients and the hospital might be eligible. At one of the earliest meetings, was read a letter from the Ministry of Pensions suggesting a capitation grant of 9s. 9d. per week per paraplegic case. The Chairman was asked to respond requesting a grant of 11s.

The British Red Cross Society also had a fundamental role to play in the funding. When, in 1920, Mr. Charrington agreed to offer the house for a further 15 months, the Society was approached with an appeal for a grant from December 1920 to enable the Hospital to carry on until March 1922. This uncertainty, which the hospital had to cope with, was to be a continuing difficulty. The response to this appeal was the granting of the sum of £12,000. The Hospital Committee asked the Society if the whole or part of the grant could be paid immediately, as the funds available to the Committee at that time would not carry them through until the end of September. This met with an unwelcome response, for the Society stated that they had understood that the grant would not be required until January 1921; as this was not the case, the appeal would have to be re-considered. However, in September £3,000 was received, no doubt to the great relief, albeit temporarily, of the Committee members. A further £3,000 arrived in November and £6,000 in the following January. This therefore honoured the original grant, and Sir Basil Mayhew, of the Joint War Finance Committee, indicated that it would be in order for the hospital to make a further application for grants after the autumn of 1921, when the original grant would have been used.

When the autumn came, Sir Arthur Stanley told the Committee that this matter had come up before the Joint War Council. That Council had deferred their decision until the 'Star and Garter' committee had been consulted as to whether they were in a position to find the necessary funds with which to pay the annual sums required for the maintenance of Gifford House. (The 'Star and Garter' referred to is, of course, the now well known Home for Disabled Ex-Servicemen at Richmond in Surrey. It was originally established in 1916 to relieve the overcrowding in military hospitals. With the generous help of the Auctioneers and Estate Agents Institute, the old *Star and Garter Hotel* on Richmond Hill was bought and presented to H.M. Queen Mary. The building was, however, soon found to be too small for the increasing demands, and it was decided to erect a larger and more suitable hospital on the site. Built into the very top of Richmond Hill and facing down the slope to the lovely loop of the River Thames, it was designed by Sir Edwin Cooper, who gave his services without charge, to accommodate 200 patients and the necessary resident staff. Funds for the project came from many sources, but the main donors were the Women of Britain and of the Empire, whose special war memorial it is. This vast E-shaped neo-Georgian building in pleasant red brick was eventually opened in July 1924 by King George V and Queen Mary. In 1953 Her Majesty the Queen became the Patron of the Home. It is probably fair to say that it is today one of the most famous homes for ex-servicemen, remaining an independent charity and in many respects similar to Gifford House.)

The 'Star and Garter' committee subsequently stated that they were unable to provide such funds. The Joint War Finance Committee decided that they would find a sum not exceeding £10,000 per annum until the new 'Star and Garter' hospital was ready to receive patients from Gifford House. Somewhat enigmatically, a minute then records that 'the future of the Hospital after March 1923 (when the loan of Gifford House expires) was fully discussed'. With concern and anxiety laced with realism, no doubt, and perhaps the Chaplain was asked to use his own 'contacts' to this end!

One of the factors which emerged as the result of the need to guarantee the financial status of the hospital was to consider whether it should be classified as a 'Red Cross' hospital. This is one of the suggestions discussed with Sir Arthur Stanley by Mrs. Hay, largely in recognition of the financial assistance given by the British Red Cross Society. The constitution of the hospital would remain unaltered and Colonel Badeley indicated that, in his opinion, the hospital already conformed with the war-time conditions of a Red Cross hospital in, for example, the way in which it submitted its accounts to Headquarters. All this began to pale, however, when in 1923 more radical aspects claimed the Committee's attention.

There had always been in the background a sense of impermanence about Gifford House solely because the premises had been lent to the hospital on a temporary basis, renewable yearly. Suddenly this was changed by the offer from Mr. Charrington to sell to the Queen Alexandra Hospital Home Gifford House and about 14 acres of grounds for the sum of £30,000 (£600,000). The Committee were receptive to this proposal because of their wish to guarantee the permanence of the Hospital Home in memory of Lady Ripon. It was thought advisable, first, to have the property valued, and Mr. Fladgate undertook to arrange this. He engaged the services of a Mr. Vigers whose report was favourable, and recommended that, in view of the purposes to which the building would be put, the sum of £30,000 was indeed reasonable.

So the future of Gifford House had to be fully discussed. Sir Arthur Stanley thought that it was premature to come to a decision, for the Star and Garter would not be ready for another year or more and this could affect the viability of the project. Prudently, the Committee asked Sir Lisle Webb if he could let the Committee know the number of beds likely to be required for men 80 per cent-100 per cent disabled at the end of 1924, i.e. in 18 months' time. In February 1924, Mrs. Hay had a meeting with Sir Arthur Stanley who told her that he had been able to spend one Sunday at Sandgate (i.e. the Star and Garter home which was situated in the area called Sandgate on Richmond Hill; the Chairman of Sandgate Urban District Council was one of the original Vice-Presidents). He had talked to the men there; with only two or three exceptions, they had expressed unhappiness at the prospect of being transferred to the new Star and Garter at Richmond. Their main concern was that they would not be able to continue their hobbies, e.g. poultry-keeping and pigeons which gave them so much pleasure at Sandgate. Sir Arthur stated that 'the men shall not leave Sandgate any more than your men shall leave Gifford House'. Something must be done to make this possible. If indeed they had made a mistake about the Star and Garter, he did not wish the men to suffer for it. He authorised Mrs. Hay to see Mr. Charrington as soon as possible. She was to ask him whether he would accept a lower price. Sir Arthur also asked her to use her influence with the Ministry of Pensions with regard to cases with which to fill the Star and Garter.

35   *Lady Juliet Duff*

Mrs. Hay's meeting with Mr. Charrington found him unyielding on the price, but Mrs. Hay expressed to the Committee her opinion that if Mr. Charrington were given a definite offer 'Mrs. Charrington would persuade him to accept as she is most anxious that the house should be sold'!

In the meantime, a report from the medical officer declared that, whilst the general health of the patients was satisfactory, the uncertainty about the future of Gifford House was causing a number of them considerable anxiety.

On 1 May 1924, Mrs. Hay and Lady Juliet Duff met Sir Arthur who informed them that the Joint War Finance Committee of the Order of St John and the British Red Cross Society would not undertake to help towards the maintenance of Gifford House after 1 September that year. He had therefore broached the matter with the main Red Cross committee which had voted the sum of £8,000 for one year from September. He suggested that Mrs. Hay should approach the Ministry of

Pensions to see if they would be willing to pay all the maintenance expenses, in which case he might be able to take some steps towards seeing if anything could be done towards the purchase of Gifford House. The offer of £8,000 was quite unsatisfactory. Not only did it leave unanswered the question of maintenance after September 1925 but Mr. Charrington had only agreed to lend Gifford House until such time as the Star and Garter was ready to receive patients. Thus the Committee found themselves between a rock and a hard place.

Another tactic was suggested. £30,000 was due to be spent on enlarging the Star and Garter home at Sandgate, but if the Ministry of Pensions did not require more beds there, might it be possible to appeal to the Star and Garter committee to obtain the sanction of the Charity Commissioners to use some of this money for the purchase of Gifford House? Sir William Goschen had been told by the Minister of Pensions, Mr. Roberts, that he intended to visit the Star and Garter home to see if it were suitable for paraplegic patients. The Committee decided to await the outcome of the letter which was expected from Mr. Roberts.

They did not have long to wait, and the reply was in their favour. The Minister had visited, as intended, and in his opinion the Star and Garter home was not suitable for paraplegics, due to the difficulty of nursing in single rooms, the underground workshops, the position of the building at the top of Richmond Hill and the lack of grounds. He urged the Committee to make further representations to the Joint War Finance Committee to make a grant so that Gifford House could continue. Sir William Goschen therefore met Sir Robert Hudson who gave his permission for Sir William to bring the matter before the next meeting of the Joint War Finance Committee on 15 May. In the meantime there had still been no official notification from the Red Cross about the £8,000 which had supposedly been voted for the maintenance of Gifford House.

In June, Sir William was able to report that the Joint War Finance Committee had indeed discussed the question of the future of Gifford House. He and Sir Arthur Stanley were deputed to have an interview with the Ministry of Pensions to put the question of whether or not the Ministry would still make the capitation grant if Gifford House were to continue. Sir Arthur was not able to be at the meeting but Sir William was able to discuss the matter with Sir Lisle Webb and the head of the Finance Branch. The latter's message was that the Treasury would not sanction any increase in the capitation grant.

At a subsequent meeting, the Joint War Finance Committee cast doubts on the evidence for the unsuitability of the Star and Garter accommodation, describing it as 'lay evidence'. Certainly it was insufficient for the Committee even to consider rescinding its decision about the conditions attached to their grant. On the other hand, they did not want to be a party to the removal of the patients from Gifford House until the Medical Staff of the Star and Garter were able to give the assurance that the accommodation was indeed suitable for paraplegic patients.

Meantime, reported Mrs. Hay, more money was needed in order to be able to carry on until the end of September and an application for a further £2,000 was made. Perhaps with relief that some decisions were still within their power, the Committee authorised repairs to a hutted ward (£10), an alteration to the kitchen ventilation and the draining of the lake for £25; hopefully this gave the members some satisfaction.

By January 1925 no report had been received from the medical staff about the suitability of the Star and Garter accommodation for the paraplegic and heavy cases at Gifford House. Mrs. Hay had had a negative response from the Treasury about the request to increase the capitation grant. She attended a meeting with Sir Lisle Webb to see if the Treasury would instead give a special maintenance grant over and above the capitation grant. Then came some brighter news. Sir William was able to report that the Joint War Finance Committee had fully discussed the future of Gifford House. In view of the representations from the Ministry of

Pensions, it was finally agreed that the Treasury would give a special maintenance grant of £2,000 per year. The Joint War Finance Committee promised a yearly grant of £6,000 for a period not exceeding six years. One can imagine that there will have been cheers of jubilation from the Committee members who can have rightly felt that their persistent lobbying had yielded dividends.

Such joy was not entirely undiluted for there were conditions to be met (could one have expected it to be otherwise?). The first was that no fresh cases were to be admitted to Gifford House. Mrs. Hay (one supposes in a sense of some indignation) pointed out that this was most unreasonable. She and Sir Lisle Webb attended a meeting of the Joint War Finance Committee on 16 December to put this very point, but the Committee refused to budge.

Mrs. Hay now wrote to Mr. Charrington to let him know that, subject to certain conditions, the maintenance of Gifford House was assured for up to six years. Would he be prepared to accept a substantial rent or a sum down for this period? His response at an interview with Mrs. Hay was that he did not wish to accept any payment and indeed would be pleased to continue to lend Gifford House indefinitely—unless he got a very good offer for it. (How did Mrs. Hay feel about that comment?)

Negotiations continued, the most satisfactory outcome of which was that the Joint War Finance Committee modified its condition about the admission of fresh patients. Based on a letter dated 8 June 1925 signed by Sir Arthur Stanley (on behalf of the Joint War Committee) and Major George Stanley (on behalf of the Ministry of Pensions), the final agreement was accepted. The chief conditions were:

1. That the annual deficiency on the maintenance account be contributed up to a sum of £8,000—by the Finance Committee of the British Red Cross Society and Order of St John, and the Ministry of Pensions in the proportion of 6 to 2 respectively with effect from 1 January 1925.
2. That this sum be apportioned per head over an agreed list of paraplegic patients to be taken as at 1 January 1925.
3. That as any 'listed' patient dies or leaves, a proportionate reduction be made in the respective contributions: listed patients temporarily returning to the Hospital, together with old paraplegic patients discharged prior to 1 January 1925 to be admitted for further treatment, to be re-instated on the list.
4. That the liability of the Ministry of Pensions and Joint War Committee shall cease at the end of the sixth year from 1 January 1925, or earlier if the Hospital is closed, or if for any other reason, it is considered desirable or necessary.

Separately, the Joint War Committee agreed to pay their grant quarterly in advance, and the Ministry of Pensions monthly in arrears, an arrangement which proved to work very satisfactorily.

This was a very significant victory for Mrs. Hay and the members of the Committee. It guaranteed, as far as was possible, the future of Gifford House by demolishing any proposal that it should merge with any other similar body, thus perpetuating the memorial to Lady Ripon. Secondly, it ensured that the Ministry accepted financial responsibility for all the patients who came within their remit, thus enabling a flow of capitation monies to reach Gifford House. And the link with the British Red Cross was strengthened to the considerable benefit of both parties. Whilst this account has been very much blow-by-blow related, the reader will see not only the gains but also how devastating would have been the failure to negotiate such agreements; certainly the very existence of the home would have been seriously threatened.

At this point, in December 1925, we must refer back to an emergency meeting of the Executive Committee which was held on 24 January 1923, for it was not only unusual in nature but highly significant in its results.

The meeting was held at 16 Upper Brook Street, the home of Lady Juliet Duff, who was in the chair. She had a matter of considerable import to communicate to the Committee. The full minute goes as follows:

> The Chairman stated that Mrs. Hay had informed her that she very much regretted that she might be unable to continue to act as Hon. Secretary and Commandant of the Hospital, as owing to the general increase in expenses and to taxation, she had to contemplate leaving London and living in the country. The Chairman stated that a meeting of the Committee had been held and the Committee was unanimously of the opinion that it was most undesirable that Mrs. Hay should sever her connection with the Hospital, where she was doing indispensable work and it had been suggested to Mrs. Hay that they would be prepared to pay her an expense allowance at the rate of £300 per annum to take effect from 1 January 1922.

Mrs. Hay had informed her that with this remuneration she would still be able to live in London and continue her work for the Hospital and it was thereupon resolved, on the proposition of the Chairman, seconded by Mr. Fladgate, to vote a sum of £300 per annum to Mrs. Hay for her services to the Hospital, with effect from 1 January 1922.

It was left to the Chairman of the Finance Committee to make arrangements for the payment of the allowance for 1922 forthwith and the remuneration for the current year by quarterly instalments.

Whatever the reasons for the plight in which Mrs. Hay found herself, and however unusual the decision of the Committee might seem to have been, this chapter itself will be a testimony to the contribution which she made to the early wellbeing of Gifford House and which was to be renewed many times over. The confidence which was placed in her was amply rewarded.

CHAPTER 7

◆

THE FINANCIAL TIGHTROPE

The detailed handling and oversight of the finances of Gifford House were placed under the care of a Finance Committee. The minutes of the meetings were kept in manuscript and the hand is identical from the third meeting onwards. The accounts of the Memorial Fund were to be kept quite separate from those of the hospital and also for the Compassionate Fund or any related recreational activities. The records of the maintenance accounts for the hospital were kept according to the rules set out in the 'Uniform System of Accounts for Hospitals'. An inventory was taken showing property which belonged to the Hospital, the Order of St John and the owners of the property respectively. The Matron was to be responsible for placing all supply orders and the doctor for the medical supplies. Systems were established for the handling of supplies, the cost of maintenance, and the supervision of work; procedures for petty cash and cheque handling were agreed and the statements of expenditure etc. which must be prepared for each committee and the dates for submission. This may sound rather mundane but it is important to realise that the finances of the Hospital were always under strict control, highly necessary as the life of the hospital evolved. The statistical returns were precisely specified and it is just a little galling that these are nowhere to be found in existing records. However, as we see how the hospital develops, the size of the enterprise will gradually emerge and we shall be able to get a fascinating insight into the costs involved and the difficulties which were faced in the financial sphere.

The role of Mrs. Hay was very clearly specified from the start, namely to attend all Finance meetings in her capacity as Chairman of the House Committee and to act as Honorary Organising Secretary of the Memorial Fund. This may seem unexceptional until one looks at what this meant in terms of her commitment to the cause which was so dear to her. One set of statistics will serve to illustrate this: of the first 100 meetings of the Finance Committee, Mrs. Hay attended 90 and this excludes nine meetings where the minutes did not state who attended. These meetings took place from April 1919 to December 1928, mostly at her home at 17 Chester Square, London. At the same time, she was expected to attend the meetings of the Executive Committee and over the same period of time she missed none of the 30 meetings held (with one exception which will be described later). It is significant that the welfare of the hospital should be so dependent upon one person but it is even more significant that Mrs. Hay carried out her responsibilities with such commitment and energy and devotion. (One can present a case which shows how true this has been throughout its history and it is appropriate that the

36 *Mrs. Hay watching a printing demonstration*

distinguished service of Mrs. Hay and many of her successors should be recognised as we follow through their work in the coming pages.)

The state of the finances in 1919 is instructive. A financial statement was prepared as at 20 May in that year and was as follows:

	£	s.	d.	£	s.	d.
Cash at Bankers and In Hand						
At Bankers Messrs. Cox & Co. No1 Account						
Current Account	2,723	4	9			
Deposit Account	2,900	0	0	5,623	4	9
No2 Account						
Current Account	173	10	4			
Deposit Account	14,000	0	0	14,173	10	4
Barclay's Bank Ltd Roehampton				360	0	0
				20,156	15	1
Cash in hand (as per Matron's Petty Cash Book)				2	12	6
				20,159	7	7

To relate these sums in today's values, the amounts above should be multiplied by twenty. Even so, a financial base of just over £400,000 seems a remarkably fragile one upon which to launch such a venture. As the story unfolds, it will be seen that the fragility of the finances was never far from the top of the agenda of the various committees, which makes their performance in ensuring the viability of the hospital all the more laudable. Again we note that Gifford House has been served by some very dedicated people.

However tight the financial situation may have been, it must be stressed that this was not allowed to get in the way of providing care for patients even if their own financial situation or that of their sponsor threatened their ongoing care. Two examples will suffice. At the meeting of the Finance Committee on 20 February 1923 the following minute is recorded: 'Authority was given to keep Butler in the Hospital without capitation grant' and on 14 March 1928: 'It was resolved that Pensioner Fleming be retained as a patient notwithstanding the cessation of payment on his behalf by the Joint War Committee'.

We know no more than these rather bald facts about both patients. Doubtless the entitlements had ceased legitimately and so the question of funding for their continuance in the Hospital would have been one to cause them concern. At the time of Butler's case, the cost of maintaining a bed was £91 per year. Records exist of payments by individuals on behalf of patients, so presumably in the cases mentioned above there was no other support upon which to call; those were times when social and other benefits were scarce or non-existent in comparison to today's systems. But the principle at issue was a serious one. In November 1921 a letter was received from the Joint War Committee promising support to the hospital 'within reasonable limits' underlining what the Governors knew to be patently true—that the income could never be guaranteed to a particular level, and certainly not to the level of expenditure. In 1926 this concern was minuted: 'the maintenance contributions from the Joint War Committee and the Ministry of Pensions will become less as patients die, or leave the hospital, with the result that, in course of time, maintenance expenditure will tend to exceed receipts'.

It is quite instructive to examine the accounts of the earlier days in terms of the items which were being purchased and also the costs involved, most of which seem to the modern reader to be ridiculously low. The earliest account for the patients' uniforms—the 'hospital blues'—dates from

37 *Some of the Ballroom patients and staff*

May 1919 when Messrs. J. & B. Pearse and Co. submitted an invoice for £159 16s. 0d. for blue serge jackets, vests and trousers. (Alas we do not know how many were supplied with this order.) But payment of this invoice was deferred until the goods could be thoroughly checked, a mark of good housekeeping which we shall see repeated.

In July of the same year we see that one of the revolving shelters from the roof of the King George Hospital in Waterloo was removed to Gifford House. The sum of £28 15s. 0d. was paid for this asset and its transport to Roehampton cost a further 7s. 6d. The next item approved was for bedsteads (how many?) provided by Harrods at a cost of £93 13s. 0d.

Continuing the clothing costs, ties were provided (one invoice was for £5. 8s. 0d.) as were hats—for the princely sum of £17 5s. 0d. (again we do not know how many). Overcoats were bought to the value of £110.

An item of a more permanent nature was the provision of a crockery store in 1921, the contents of which were purchased for £35 13s. 8d. A Roneo copying machine was also acquired; it would seem that technological advances were used where the benefits were measurable.

In the area of maintenance, we find an item in 1923 for the re-decoration of the bathrooms and the installation of a new bath for the total sum of £20!

Some memories may be stirred by the way in which bills from the electricity and water companies were rendered for supply to 'Michaelmas' or 'Lady Day'; those days in the calendar would have meant much more than in modern times. The quarterly electricity bill was around £53 and water £18; the half-yearly rates were £64. (In 1996 the average quarterly electricity bill was £3,750 but this does include a much higher electricity usage for modern treatment equipment and improved lighting levels.)

As mentioned earlier, the accounts were vetted thoroughly before payment. For example, a 1920 bill for £25 0s. 6d. for chimney sweeping was considered to be excessive; the supplier was asked to reduce his charge by £5 and Mrs Hay undertook to arrange with another firm to carry out the work in future. Nor did the Wandsworth Borough Council escape this conscientious approach; the Committee received a letter in June 1921 'intimating that the Council would be prepared to accept payment of one half of the Rates due, in satisfaction of their demand'; this was duly paid in the following month. The principle was also applied to major purchases. In June 1924, authority was given for 'the purchase of furniture and bedding at two forthcoming auction sales, the expenditure not to exceed £125'. Similarly, an eagle eye seems to have been kept on costs; we find a Minute authorising the 'expenditure necessary to fill the coal cellars at summer prices'—and few would criticise this conscientious approach to purchasing. There was one apparently parsimonious ruling which was not well received at the time; in May 1921, Mrs Hay was asked 'to request the members of the staff to refrain from using the telephone unless in cases of emergency, and it was further resolved that a charge of 2d. per call be made when the telephone is so used'.

It does seem that in the question of salaries and remuneration, the Committee was fair-handed. But the records show first a rather surprising approach to the payment process. As early as the fourth meeting of the Finance Committee it was resolved that as the payment of monthly salaries by cheque 'involved considerable unnecessary labour ... that in future all salaries, except the Matron's and the Medical Officer's, should be paid in cash, one cheque being drawn for the total sum'. This seems a little strange, as anyone who has had to coin up for military pay parades will know the effort involved; subsequent moves to bank transfers have meant much saving of time.

What were the salaries for the staff? These seem to have been developed on an *ad hoc* basis at first but in April 1919 a full scheme was agreed by the Committee. This took the form of a revision of the rates of pay which had been carried out by Mrs. Hay. Her recommendations were as follows:

That from 1 May 1921 the rates of pay should be:

Matron	£135 per annum
	Annual increment £10
Housekeeper }	£100 per annum
Secretary }	Annual increment £5
Sisters: 1st and 2nd years	£75 per annum
3rd year	£85 per annum
	Then annual increment £5
Permanent night Sisters	£80 per annum
Nurses	£38 per annum
	Annual increment £2 10s. 0d.
	Maximum £43
Accountant	£75 per annum

With the introduction of these rates the previous system of bonus payments was to be scrapped. The proposals were accepted.

The monthly meetings approved each time the payments to the Resident Medical Officer of £58 6s. 8d. per month and £12 10s. 0d. to the Chaplain. A year later, Matron's salary was increased to the maximum of £150 and this was in line with the way in which the Committee consistently followed its agreed bonus policy. It also carried out reviews of salary levels and towards the end of 1923 the annual salary for Sisters was raised to £90 and for the Cook to £100. (One assumes that their comparative scales were not public knowledge!) Good news again for the Matron early in 1924 when it was 'unanimously resolved that in view of the excellent services of the Matron, Miss L. Fletcher, and the Secretary, Miss W. E. Bush, their salaries be raised as from 1 January to £200 and £130 per annum' respectively with 'a further bonus to the secretary of £20 in respect of the year 1923'.

The consideration of the appropriate levels of remuneration took some interesting courses over the years. The wish to recognise performance was a continuing theme of the Committee

38 *Out of uniform—a Fancy Dress Party*

meetings. For example, in March 1925 the following was minuted: 'In the special circumstances explained by Mrs. Hay it was resolved that a special grant of £5, in respect of salary be made to Sister Murrell' which presumably was based upon special circumstances of a confidential nature. Yet only five months previously, Mrs. Hay 'raised the question of the wages paid to the orderlies, with a view to an enquiry as to whether future engagements could be made at a lower rate. It was resolved to enquire as to the wages paid to orderlies at the Star and Garter'.

In 1926 it was the turn of the massage staff to come under the microscope. The Committee decided that from March in that year the weekly rate of pay for men and women should be £2 2s. 0d. and that the mid-day meal should no longer be supplied. This was not well received by the staff for at the following meeting it was recorded that 'letters were read from the Massage staffs regarding the remuneration arrangements: the Committee re-affirmed the decision arrived at last month'. Yet individual cases were treated with understanding. One of the male nurses, Mr. York, had been off duty through sickness for four months and on his return to duty it was agreed that the payment of his full salary during that time should be made. Interestingly, it had been one of the earliest decisions of the main House Committee that each male nurse should be granted a gratuity not exceeding £10 upon his taking annual leave; this could be regarded as sensitive personnel management in days when automatic entitlement to holiday pay was for many merely a chimera. Similarly, the executive committee ruled that uniform dresses be supplied to Sisters and that two dresses each

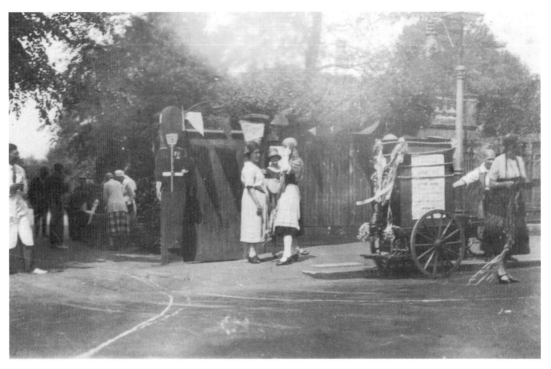

39   *Fund-raising with a hurdy-gurdy outside the gates—and a cut-out guardsman*

year be supplied to each nurse after two years' service. A balance had to be struck between responsible financial management and equitable people-handling; judging by the ongoing tone of the minutes there was little need to respond to grievances. One episode does leave us curious about the circumstances. A rather terse minute in November 1920 records that 'the House Committee had given the lodgekeeper a fortnight's notice'. Three months later, Mrs Hay reported that the lodgekeeper (whose pay was 35s. per week) had been unable to obtain other work or accommodation—'it was agreed therefore that the present arrangements should continue'.

But other matters also claimed the attention of the Committee. Not surprisingly, the most frequent matters for discussion concerned the maintenance of the building. One of the more frequent suppliers was Waygood Otis who were regularly summoned to attend to the lift. In January 1921 the large boiler burst and a replacement was installed as soon as possible, the matter being reported to the Committee *post factum*. Only nine months later, Mrs Hay told the Committee that a further section had burst and that a recent storm had caused serious damage to the conservatory. Then the steamer gave up the ghost, necessitating the purchase of a replacement for £72 with a monthly inspection of the apparatus at a monthly fee of 26s. The need to arrange to have the fire extinguishers tested periodically was noted … and anyone who has ever had any responsibility for buildings and their maintenance will merely comment: Business as usual!

We can best leave at this point these details of domestic concern; not that they can be ignored, for however well motivated anyone may be about a project (and that was certainly the case for Mrs. Hay and her team) the practical effects of decisions have to be faced, day-to-day detail being one that will never go away.

A brief return to our note of caution which has sounded throughout this chapter—the overall sensitivity about the constraints on finance. This theme appears in the minutes of November 1921:

'A letter from the Joint War Committee, promising the support of the Hospital "within reasonable limits" was submitted'. Precisely; the income of the Hospital could never be guaranteed at a certain level (nor can it today). Hence a few months later, Sir Reginald Cox undertook to 'make enquiries regarding the investment of moneys standing on the Memorial Fund Deposit Account', a natural enough task when income has to be maximised from all possible sources. And a minute from January 1926 can be an even stronger note to lead us into the situation which the main House Committee had often to face:

> It was resolved that, having in view that the maintenance contributions from the Joint War Committee and the Ministry of Pensions will become less as patients die, or leave the Hospital, with the result that, in course of time maintenance expenditure will tend to exceed receipts, it is resolved that the moneys received from the Bazaar organised by Lady Juliet [Duff] together with sundry donations since received and placed to the same account be made a separate Fund; that Mrs. Hay be given power to allocate to such Fund any donations received and not otherwise allocated, and that the Fund be available, as and when need arises, to make good any deficiency on Maintenance account.

The pattern of financial control will continue to be careful attention to detail within an overall strategy.

CHAPTER 8

♦

NEGOTIATIONS FOR THE MOVE TO WORTHING

The arrangements which we read about in chapter six concerning the reasonable guarantee of the future of Gifford House inevitably began to run out of time and it was necessary to take up the cudgels again with the authorities. To be specific, the main target of the Governors was the Ministry of Pensions, although there was never any trace of acrimony. The Governors found a strong ally in the Joint War Council and were able to gain a further benefactor in the Royal Savoy Association.

By the middle of 1930, with six months of the agreement of 8 June 1925 still to run, they began their internal discussions. Efforts were already under way to gain the support of the Joint War Council (viz., the British Red Cross and the Order of St John of Jerusalem). Sir William Goschen had an interview with Sir Basil Mayhew of the Joint War Finance Committee. Ammunition consisted in memoranda he had received from the Minister of Pensions, the former minister Mr. Roberts, Major Tryon, Sir E. Farquhar Buzzard and Sir Lisle Webb. These documents strongly urged that everything possible should be done to carry on the work as long as Mr. Charrington was willing to lend Gifford House.

As part of the public relations approach, all members of the Joint War Finance Committee were invited to attend the Garden Fete on 26 June; Lady Juliet Duff also agreed to send copies of Mrs. Hay's memorandum which set out the case for the renewal of the grant from the government. Lady Juliet proposed a meeting with Sir Arthur Stanley so that she and Mrs. Hay could make a personal approach to gain his support.

By January 1931 no response had been received about either the capitation grant from the Joint War Finance Committee or the Special Grant from the Ministry of Pensions. There had been some discussions in December but the proposals were thought to be financially unworkable. Part of the difficulty was the number of patients on the 'agreed list'. These were the patients whom the Ministry had agreed to support as long as they were eligible. Mrs. Hay wanted to add a further 23 names to the list; those were patients who had been admitted since January 1926 and for whom the Ministry was responsible. The Joint War Finance Committee agreed in principle.

At this point, mention is made in the minutes of the Executive Committee, of the Royal Savoy Association Seaside Holiday Home, a report on which had previously been circulated to them. There had been no meeting of the Executive Committee since the previous June and so we have to conclude that, during that time, the need to search for a permanent home had become established in the minds of the Governors. Presumably, too, they had had informal discussions with the Royal Savoy Association about their ideas. They certainly felt it necessary to notify the Association about their search for a suitable property. What was this charity and how did its potential affect the future of Gifford House?

The Royal Savoy Association was a charity which had been inaugurated during the war by the Revd. Hugh Chapman and was registered under the War Charities Act, 1916 to help our prisoners in Germany. After the war ended, it obtained permission to direct its attention to the relief of paralysed soldiers and sailors. In fact, Mrs. Hay was at a meeting of the Association as early as 17 February 1919 accounting to them about how any grant they might make to Gifford House would be spent.

40   *Patients at the Eastbourne holiday home*

On 16 February 1922 she told them that she would like to have a grant of £500 to send 20 patients from Gifford House for a month's holiday to the seaside, five at a time with a Sister, nurse and orderly. These patients were paralysed men who could never hope for a holiday owing to their disabilities and the constant nursing required, and who saw their more mobile fellow patients re-turning to their own homes for a month's leave (by the sanction of the Ministry of Pensions). The holiday home was at Eastbourne, the destination of the three valiant auto-wheel adventurers.

The Association readily granted £250 and indeed suggested that the Governors of Gifford House would in due course need further financial assistance. The Hon. Treasurer was the 8th Duke of Richmond and Gordon (at that time Lord March) and he wrote to the *Times* appealing for donations for this cause. The response, together with the holiday fund already held by Gifford House, enabled 25 patients to benefit in the first year. The Duke became increasingly interested in this work and the fund grew steadily year by year. This meant that a further category of men could be included, namely those who had returned to their homes after being patients at either the King George Hospital or Gifford House. The first beneficiaries were 12 paralysed and eight totally disabled patients who, although they had 100 per cent pensions, found no margin in that sum for a holiday or a change of environment, and who found it extremely difficult to go anywhere in their chairs. Needless to say, the others to benefit were their wives who had to care for them and who could thereby have a rest from their responsibilities knowing that their husbands were being cared for by fully trained nursing staff. When the Duke wrote to the *Daily Mail* in 1926, many War case disabled men contacted him, and in that year nearly 70 men benefited, including 20 from Gifford House. It was therefore a sensible marriage for the two charities to contemplate.

When the Governors met on 5 May 1932, surprisingly not having had a meeting for the past 16 months, members of the Royal Savoy Association were present for the first time, so a considerable amount of informal contact was beginning to bear fruit. Also present was Mr. W. Oates, a founder member of the Wimbledon Branch of the 'Lest-We-Forget' Association; he had a motor business in Wimbledon, had shown a great interest in Gifford House and he was to render sterling service of a very practical nature during the move to Worthing. All those present had seen beforehand the proposals for the grants which had been agreed by the Joint War Finance Committee and the Ministry of Pensions and contained in a letter from Sir Basil Mayhew for the Joint War Finance Committee and Sir George Chrystal on behalf of the Ministry of Pensions. It was addressed to Mrs. Hay:

Dear Madam,

    We are desired by the Minister of Pensions and the Joint War Finance Committee of the British Red Cross Society and the Order of St John of Jerusalem to inform you that they have agreed to co-operate with each other for a further period in financing the Queen Alexandra Hospital, Gifford House, Roehampton, on the same basis as under the agreement of June 1925, subject to the following conditions and modifications:-

1. The Hospital shall not continue beyond a period of two years as from 1st January 1931, save in the circumstances referred to in 8.

2. By that date all patients shall be dispersed to other Homes or Hospitals.

3. Names which shall be approved by the Ministry and selected from those cases in respect of which a capitation rate of 11s. per day is now payable may be added to the Agreed List from time to time provided that the List shall not at any time exceed 40 names.

4. No financial responsibility shall fall upon the Ministry or Joint Committee in respect of dilapidations or reinstatement of Gifford House on the closing of the Hospital or any expenses not connected with the maintenance or treatment of Ministry Patients.

5. In the event of the Hospital Committee securing a Seaside Holiday Home within the period of two years as has been suggested the survivors of the Agreed List (being the list of original patients agreed to in the year 1925 and as hereby amended) shall be sent thereto by the Ministry as patients if the conditions are regarded by the Ministry as suitable but the agreed list shall not be added to after the Hospital is closed.

6. The Ministry agrees not to send to the Holiday Home as permanent patients any other cases except with the agreement of the Joint Committee.

7. The Ministry agrees to pay for its permanent patients whose maintenance is a charge upon the Ministry capitation rates not exceeding 11s. or 7s. a day as may be appropriate according to the class of patient but the Ministry reserves the right to review these rates after Gifford House is closed so that the rates may be in accord with those rates which may be paid for similar classes of patients residing in Red Cross institutions. The financial responsibility of the Ministry in respect of the proposed Holiday Home shall be strictly limited to the payment of the capitation rates referred to.

8. In the event of the project for a Seaside Holiday Home being abandoned or delayed, the provisions of the agreement may be extended for a further period but not beyond 30th June 1933.

9. The accumulated balance on Income and Expenditure account at 31st December 1930, amounting to £3,974. 5s. 6d. shall be regarded as belonging to the parties hereto in the following proportions:-

Hospital Committee	£2,988.	3s.	0d.
Joint War Committee	£739.	11s.	10d.
Ministry of Pensions	£246.	10s.	8d.
	£3,974.	5s.	6d.

Perhaps you will be good enough to confirm at an early date that the foregoing arrangements meet with the approval of your Committee.

Some very important points of principle had been agreed in the Governors' favour, though not to the detriment of any other party. The agreement to continue on this basis gave them two years in which to realise their dream of a seaside holiday home, whilst at the same time guaranteeing the financial stability of the home. The agreed list was indeed expanded, the capitation rates were satisfactory and the right to refuse patients was established. Finally, the time extension for a further two years, if necessary, ensured a lifeline in the event of negotiations dragging on. In summary, from this distance in time, one can only say that the Governors were extremely successful in their achievements, not only in the short term but in establishing principles regarding funding and responsibilities which are still the raft upon which the hospital runs successfully today.

In the meantime, Mrs. Hay's efforts to identify a suitable property were beginning to bear fruit. She had reported to the Finance Committee in March 1932 that she had heard of a house in Worthing which might be suitable as a permanent home in conjunction with the Royal Savoy

41 *The 8th Duke of Richmond and Gordon*

42   *'The Gables' as pictured in Patching's brochure*

Association and the Duke of Richmond and Gordon's Seaside Holiday Scheme. Indeed, she had visited the property known as 'The Gables' taking with her the Duke of Richmond and Gordon and Dr. Hebb, Director General of Medical Services in the Ministry of Pensions. They each thought that, together with additional temporary buildings and some alterations, it would be suitable for their requirements. The asking price was £9,500 but she was sure that it could be purchased for a good deal less and Sir William Goschen and the Finance Committee had empowered her to make an offer of £8,000.

Mrs. Hay put forward an offer of £7,500 to include fixtures and fittings. The Agents for the sale were Messrs Patching & Co. of 5 Chapel Road and Railway Approach, Worthing (Telephone 122). Having communicated with the owners, they came back to suggest an increase in the offer to £8,000 but Mrs. Hay decided not to increase the offer in view of the expense which would be incurred in the extra buildings. A letter to this effect was sent to the Agents, and the Executive Committee left it to her discretion whether or not to increase the offer to £8,000 in the near future. It is refreshing to read of such trust being placed in her; one cannot help feeling that this trust was well placed and that she made a doughty negotiator.

What capital finance was available for this intended purchase? The Queen Alexandra Hospital Home itself had assets totalling £23,914, of which £11,829 was in the Memorial Fund, £9,465 in Reserves and £2,620 in the Compassionate Fund. Mrs. Hay saw the benefit of the Memorial Fund being used in the purchase because there would be a great appeal in having a permanent holiday home which was funded through donations made in memory of Lady Ripon. The Royal Savoy Association could contribute £2,617 plus £144 from the holiday fund. The Governors wanted to know the likely cost of maintenance of the building. Mrs. Hay felt that it was impossible to make an exact budget at that time, but she thought that the maximum figure would be £10,000 per annum. Of that amount, 60 per cent should be recoverable from the Ministry assuming they sent 30 patients at the standard rate of capitation grant. The number of staff needed would also have to be submitted to the Committee. The minimum numbers, as laid down by the Ministry, stipulated one Matron (at £250 pa), four Sisters (at £90 pa each), 10 Nurses (£43), two male nurses, three massage staff, and five orderlies. Together with six domestic staff, the salary bill was estimated at £2,773 12s. pa. Provisions were expected to cost £2,509 per year, surgery and dispensary £700 and the total cost was forecast to be £8,962 19s. 6d.

Sir William Goschen, who was also a member of the Joint War Finance Committee, speaking as a member of this Executive Committee, thought that the Scheme should be submitted to the

Joint War Finance Committee and he felt that their response was likely to be positive. Mrs. Hay then revealed that she had already seen Sir George Chrystal and Sir Lisle Webb of the Ministry of Pensions (she was not a lady to let grass grow under her feet) who were satisfied with the way in which the Scheme was progressing. Dr. Hebb was also positive. Lady Juliet Duff had also been canvassing support, this time from Sir Arthur Stanley whom she had visited with Mrs. Hay; Sir Arthur had written her a letter of support and of his 'hearty approval'.

Mrs. Hay then asked the Committee to approve the appointment of an architect, suggesting Mr. Clyde Young so that he could deal with the alterations and additional buildings; her request was approved.

The legal aspect of the transaction now had to be addressed. The expert on the governing body was Mr. W.F. Fladgate and his contribution to the cause now became important. He reminded the Governors that when the Queen Alexandra Hospital Home was founded in 1919, it had been suggested that the Charity should be registered as a Joint Stock Company, but this had not been put into effect as the building had only been lent to them. Now that purchase of a property was being considered, the question of a Constitution must be considered. He suggested that a small Joint Stock Company, limited by guarantee of, say £1 or £5 or any sum mutually agreed upon, should be registered. Application should be made to the Board of Trade for permission to register without the word 'Limited' in the title. The company so registered would continue the work being carried on at Roehampton and the property would be conveyed to the company.

He then made a generous offer, namely that his old firm would make no charges for this work and the only expenses would therefore be Stamp Duty (at one per cent on the purchase price) and the necessary printing. His proposal and offer were heartily accepted. The Governors also decided that the land and buildings should be earmarked as being held by the Memorial Fund, to which other sums could later be transferred if necessary. This was, of course, an important principle bearing in mind the fact that Gifford House had been founded in memory of Lady Ripon. Meanwhile, although it was too early to begin detailed talks with the Royal Savoy Association, Mrs. Hay was asked to communicate with the Charity Commissioners to explain the ideas for amalgamation.

On 28 July 1932 the Governors met again to discuss the constitution for the new home and the draft Articles which had been prepared by Sir Francis Fladgate (who had received his knighthood since the last meeting. Sir Francis, whose services were in some demand was not able to attend every meeting; in July 1932 his diary was concerned with the Eton and Harrow match at Lord's and the naming of a new steamer at Sunderland by Lady Fladgate). Only that afternoon Mrs. Hay had seen Mr. W.F. Fox of the Board of Charity Commissioners and had shown him the draft Articles of Association. He proposed a simpler method, however; rather than form a company, he suggested drawing up a Scheme. This was recommended practice for the administration of any charity under the auspices of the Official Trustee who would handle any complaints made against a charity (real or imagined) and to whom the annual accounts would be submitted.

One of the matters which had to be addressed was whether or not there were any restrictions on the use of the building, a natural enough consideration bearing in mind its proximity to other dwellings. Mrs. Hay had begun to tackle this, too; could it be used other than as a private dwelling house? The original deed of 1867 could not be traced but the solicitor to the Heene Estate, Mr. Lewis Taylor, had definitely promised a Licence for 15 years for the planned purpose.

Sir Francis submitted a contract for the purchase of the property together with a schedule of tenant's fixtures and fittings. It was unanimously resolved:

1. That a letter be addressed to the Charity Commissioners asking them to prepare a Scheme on the lines suggested, for censor.

2.   That the Contract be approved, and Mrs. Hay be asked to sign it on behalf of the Committee, and be indemnified for so doing.

She promptly signed the contract and Sir Francis witnessed it.

What were they intending to buy and how did the property fit in with their concept of a hospital home? The four-page agents' brochure begins by describing Worthing as 'one of the most favoured positions on the South Coast … noted for the equability of its climate, resembling the South of France with its mild winters'. The town was at the top of the list of towns throughout the country enjoying hours of sunshine, justifying the epithet 'Sunny Worthing'. (They were diplomatic enough not to mention 'Windy Worthing'!) They praised the Southern Railway system which ran an excellent service to London, 'the distance being covered in about 80 minutes, and the service will be considerably augmented in 1933 when the line will be electrified throughout its whole length'. (In 1997, the travelling time from Worthing to Victoria was timetabled as 77 minutes for most trains.) The property was about ¾ mile from the station 'occupying a bold corner site in a matured part of the town'. A strong factor, too, was the flat nature of the promenade and sea front, which would be of great benefit for those in wheelchairs.

'The Residence' had been completed in 1888, the site having been sold in 1867 for £441 to Mr. Ralli, a Greek shipowner. The next owner was Sir Thomas Skinner, Bart. The current owners were Italian, Mr. and Mrs. Coccioletti. The house was built of 'red brick part weather tiled with tiled roof' with most of the main rooms facing south and 'completely shut off from the Domestic

43   *The Gardens of 'The Gables'*

portion'. The property was in excellent structural and decorative repair and suitable for use as a private residence or 'high-class nursing home or club, etc.'.

On the ground floor were the lounge, hall, morning room, drawing room (26ft. by 17ft. with bay), dining room (24ft. by 16ft.), study, heated winter garden and music or billiard room (28ft. by 18ft.). The rest of the ground floor was occupied by the domestic offices, including kitchen, scullery, butler's room, strong room, servants' hall and pantry, together with a bicycle house and knife house and 'good washing cellars' with a hand lift to the first floor where there were five bedrooms, one with dressing room. In the north wing were four bedrooms for staff accommodation plus three servants' bedrooms on the second floor with a tank room. The garaging was for two cars; there was stabling and a harness room with the chauffeur's living rooms over. The outbuildings included a potting shed, fodder house, bothy and a heated greenhouse. The grounds of two acres incorporated tennis, croquet and other lawns with large rose gardens and a kitchen garden. It is not difficult to understand why Mrs. Hay thought this to be so desirable a property.

Not everyone agreed with her, however. The objections which were raised came from nearby residents when they were approached about these plans. A resident who lived opposite, Colonel John Rodocanachi, had some reservations about the 'character of the buildings' which were to be erected, wondering whether the 'type of hutments' would result in 'the character of the neighbourhood and its amenities being spoilt and depreciated'. But, as Mrs. Hay pointed out in a letter whose phraseology was often repeated, 'Our men do not wear "Hospital Blue" clothes, but are always turned out neatly in navy blue serge—and no-one could take them for Institutional patients'. Not only that, but with Lord Cullen a close neighbour at Roehampton, they had never received a word of complaint from him. When Mr. Clyde Young met Colonel Rodocanachi and his sister, their fears were assuaged and they became firm supporters of the Scheme. The Colonel was most willing to meet Mrs. Hay to assure her of his goodwill: 'I am usually down at Worthing from Wednesday to Mondays. I ride most mornings, but am usually free in the afternoons or can be so, if I have advice of anyone wishing to see me'. They established a good rapport, and Miss Rodocanachi retained an interest until her death.

Mr. Goodall, another neighbour who initially supported the Scheme (and whom Mrs. Hay thought was in league with Mr. Sams, whom we shall meet below) took a different view. In a letter to the Duke of Richmond and Gordon, he wrote that he was 'not pleased at the idea of a beautiful house such as "The Gables", being turned into a home of any kind. On the other hand, I feel that no place on this earth, is too good for those who fought and were injured in serving their country … it will be rather depressing to see disabled men about in the garden; but I trust you will see to it, that no nuisance of any kind is permitted.' In another letter, dated 22 July 1932, he wrote: 'I purchased the land, and built my house, wholly for the outlook, which will be spoilt to a very large degree if other buildings are put up in the garden of "The Gables", and also it would spoil the beauty of the house, which is now quite the nicest house in Worthing'. To Mrs. Hay he was probably more honest: 'If other buildings are erected … it will take hundreds of pounds off the value of my house'. At the end of July he did meet Mrs. Hay and from that moment we hear no more from Mr. Goodall. But the most obdurate opponent was Mr. W. Sams, who lived in 'The Elms' on the east side of 'The Gables' in Boundary Road. In a letter written by Mrs. Hay, she said: 'We are up against a very cantankerous old man who lives next door to "The Gables" ' and on another occasion prophesied that he was going to be 'a hard nut to crack', which turned out to be quite correct. But assuming that they were able to take possession by the end of September 1932, the Governors decided that any local publicity should wait until then, when they would erect a board stating the purpose to which the house was to be put. At that time, the MP for Worthing would also be informed, and a suggestion put to the Mayor that a public meeting should be held in the following February so that the project could be fully explained and an appeal made for the support of local residents.

Completion of the purchase did, in fact, take place on 12 October 1932; the cost was £7,500 together with Stamp Duty of £75, and the whole sum being paid for from the Lady Ripon Memorial Fund. The property was conveyed into the names of Sir William Goschen and Sir Francis Fladgate. When Mrs. Hay had been anxious to know earlier whether or not Mr. Coccioletti would be willing to sell at their offer, but had received no reply within her preferred timescale, she confided to Sir Francis Fladgate, 'but as he is an Italian perhaps this is understandable'.

Mr. Sams then went into action, issuing a writ against them for an injunction to restrain 'The Gables' from being used as a home for disabled ex-servicemen in breach, as he saw it, of the covenants imposed on the property. Mrs. Hay had been told by a 'very old resident in Worthing' that some years previously Mr. Sams had annoyed the residents of West Worthing by putting up 'a whole market garden of glass houses behind his house and behind 'The Gables' ', and their strong objections had been over-ruled. (The glasshouses had subsequently been demolished and the land sold.) The Governors instructed Messrs Fladgate & Co. to defend such proceedings and to take all the necessary steps. Sir Francis himself did not believe that Mr. Sams would in any way be injured by either the additional buildings or the change of use of the property. Although Mr. Sams had contended that the men themselves would constitute a nuisance in the neighbourhood, that must have been considered by the local authority when they reviewed the plans; clearly they had not thought that any potential for nuisance existed. He did not think, therefore, that Mr. Sams had any case either for an injunction or for damages. He was less certain about Mr. Sams' contention about the binding nature of the covenant; if Mr. Sams did claim damages, they were likely to be minimal but, if a court adjudicated in his favour, then there might be a rather different situation. At any rate, no action should be taken until any statement of claim was received. Notwithstanding all this, the Governors were keen to adopt a policy of reconciliation, and Mrs. Hay undertook to meet the vicar of Heene, the Town Clerk (Mr. J. Kennedy Allerton) and anyone else 'who might be induced to use their influence for the good of the Home'. This latter gentlemen did his best to fit in an appointment in a very busy diary by suggesting that they met at about five o'clock at the Burlington Hotel (where Mrs. Hay was staying): 'We could then have a chat and perhaps you would be kind enough to give me a cup of tea?' She had written to him a very persuasive letter in the name of the Duke of Richmond and Gordon:

> His Grace understands that the plans have been kept to lay before a special Meeting of your Town Planning Committee … and he begs that you will ask them to give his Scheme their most sympathetic consideration; remembering that though the din and dust of war have long since died away, the sufferers— the real sufferers—are still with us. It is these men—who have been under our care for so many years—that we hope and trust to comfortably establish at 'The Gables' for the rest of their lives.

Mrs. Hay subsequently received a letter from Mr. Allerton, which stated that at its meeting on 25 October the Town Council had approved the recommendation of the Housing and Town Planning Committee, which set straightforward conditions about sanitary arrangements, ingress and egress and setting a limit of 15 years on the permission for the temporary buildings; a further condition was that the licence in respect of these temporary buildings would expire immediately the buildings ceased to be used for their intended purpose. He asked for the architect to submit detailed plans. Such plans had already been agreed by Sir Lisle Webb and Dr. Hebb of the Ministry of Pensions and Sir Basil Mayhew of the Joint War Finance Committee.

On the suggestion of the Duke of Richmond and Gordon it was agreed that from now on the two charities would hold combined meetings although the accounts would have to remain separate until the Charity Commissioners approved the Scheme. The Executive Committee also gave full powers to the Finance Committee to act on their behalf on all matters regarding the purchase, at the same time ensuring that two members of the Royal Savoy Association were present at their meetings. It was also agreed that Mrs. Hay should interview representatives from the *Worthing Gazette* and the *Worthing Herald* to give publicity to the Scheme, and a board was to be attached at the gate announcing the purpose for which the property was to be used.

In the meantime, Mrs. Hay attempted to resolve the difficulties raised by Mr. Sams. She met the Vicar of Heene, the Revd E.A. Haviland, who was in close touch with him. The vicar thought him to be 'very nice and witty, anxious to show me his point of view and willing to hear anything on the other side', and later he was under the impression that Mr. Sams was prepared 'to make certain proposals with a view to the acquisition by the Hospital Home of his property' but as these were undefined there was no action that could immediately be taken. Mrs. Hay's husband, Algernon Hay (who was also to give valued service to Gifford House and become a friend to patients and staff alike) spoke to the vicar who reported that Mr. Sams had canvassed the other residents but had failed to enlist their support. This was valuable information as it demonstrated that Mr. Sams was the only objector. Mr. Hay also felt that Mr. Sams had mixed up 'covenants' and 'damages' in his objections; perhaps there was here a chink in his armour. Mr. Sams had written to Fladgate & Co. suggesting that the Hospital should purchase his property for £4,000 and that he should remain tenant during his life. But the Governors did not think this desirable and resolved to ask him in writing, whether he would be willing to accept either an agreed sum in cash in full satisfaction for loss in the value of his property or the deposit of security up to £4,000 'from which, on his death, the amount by which the sum realised for the sale of the property fell short of £4,000 could be made good'.

A month later the Governors were told that in spite of Mr. Hay's attempts to reassure Mr. Sams of the benefits he would gain from these ideas, he had found them unacceptable. Mrs. Hay was sure that there were no other objectors likely to present any difficulties and the Governors concluded that the best approach would be to purchase 'The Elms' outright at a price not exceeding £4,000 or at a lower figure if possible. Back she went to Mr. Sams and at the meeting of the Governors on 19 January 1933 a final agreement was reached as follows:

1. We (i.e. the Governors) to purchase 'The Elms' for £4,000, to be reduced to £3,750 if allowance be made for fair wear and tear.
2. £3,000 to remain on mortgage at 2 %.
3. The Vendor to be allowed to remain as tenant for his lifetime, at a rent equal to 2 % on the £3,000 remaining on Mortgage and 3 % on the balance. The lease to be granted for Mr. Sams' lifetime and for six months thereafter, and the Mortgage to run for a corresponding time.
4. We pay the costs of the Action in the usual way.
5. Mr. Sams will pay the Vendor's costs, and we the purchaser's costs.
6. We agree to pay £4.4s. plus Stamp duty for the costs of the mortgage.
7. Mr. Sams agrees that should we be prevented from carrying out our proposals by an objector he will re-purchase the property at the sum we pay for it if an injunction is obtained restraining us, proceedings being commenced within 12 months of the purchase of 'The Elms'.

The Executive Committee passed a cordial vote of thanks to Mr. Algernon Hay 'for his kind and valued services' in connection with these negotiations, and no doubt sighs of relief were uttered by all concerned.

Parallel to these activities, steps were being taken to consult with the Charity Commissioners about the Scheme which would bind together the two charities into a permanent constitution. Amongst other aspects, the finances of Gifford House were set out in a brief to the Charity Commissioners who would, of course, have to examine and comment upon the proposal. On 15 March 1933 the funds were as follows:

£6,688 in The Lady Ripon Memorial Fund which was a collecting fund whose purpose had always been to purchase a permanent memorial to Lady Ripon; the project for 'The Gables' clearly was within the scope of this fund.

£9,430 in the Maintenance Reserve Fund, started in 1924 from the proceeds of the bazaar, with the intention of accumulating a fund for the general maintenance of the Home should the grant from the Joint War Finance Committee be reduced or discontinued.

£2,702 in the Compassionate Fund which was put to recreational and other uses for the benefit of the patients and their relatives.

£1,390 in the Worthing Home account, created temporarily from an appeal for the new building at Worthing.

£3,938 held in the account of The Royal Savoy Association.

However, not all these funds (totalling £24,148) could legitimately be used to purchase 'The Gables' due to restrictions on their use. The actual amount available for the purchase was £11,913. With the projected cost of purchase for 'The Gables' (including alterations and additions) and 'The Elms' estimated at £17,000, a deficit of £5,087 had to be covered. It was suggested that a purely temporary loan from the Maintenance Reserve Fund could achieve this but the debt would have to be cleared very quickly.

The other aspect which rightly concerned the Governors was the ongoing maintenance costs of Gifford House. As we have seen, there was a justifiable nervousness about the lack of guarantee of payment by the Ministry of Pensions of the capitation grant, both in terms of value for money and the eligibility of cases (which were the subject of close bureaucratic scrutiny). The uncertainty about the £6,000 capitation grant was based on the forecast reduction in the number of permanent patients; this was only to be expected following the cessation of hostilities. The Governors saw an increasing need to depend on voluntary contributions as well as drawing on reserves; the inclusion of funds from the Association, which its constitution permitted, would alleviate the difficulties somewhat. The expenditure was roughly estimated at £10,000. They expected the capitation grant from the Ministry of Pensions to be £6,000, the joint annual appeal to raise £1,500 and to be able to count on receiving £2,000 from the Joint War Finance Committee. A donation of £1,000 from Lady Houston was warmly welcomed, and one of the wards was later named after her.

Proposals for the newly-constituted charity were sent to the Commissioners. Leaving aside the detail necessary in such a document, two paragraphs catch the eye. One stipulated that 'there should be no Covenants to prevent the sale of the Home when its uses are finished' and it was suggested that any

44 *Dr. Oliver Gotch, Medical Officer; this photograph was taken on his retirement in 1959*

money realised should go to the Red Cross in recognition of their unflagging support. Also, that the Governors 'should be empowered to add to our property in Worthing by the purchase of small houses or cottages for the use of some of our totally disabled men'.

The Charity Commissioners duly considered the proposal and on 26 January 1934 was sealed the Scheme upon which Gifford House still operates. The detail need not concern us (the merger of the two charities was a comparatively straightforward affair) but the objects of the two charities were set out thus:

> The primary object of The Queen Alexandra Hospital Home (In Memory of Lady Ripon) shall be the maintenance of a Home or Homes for the permanent accommodation of discharged and disabled Sailors, Soldiers and Airmen of His Majesty's Forces, and the supply to the inmates of any necessary medical and surgical assistance and appliances. Subject to the primary object, and so that the carrying on of that object shall not be impaired thereby, an additional object of The Queen Alexandra Hospital Home (In Memory of Lady Ripon) shall be the accommodation in the said Home or Homes for short holidays of discharged and disabled Sailors, Soldiers and Airmen of His Majesty's Forces. The object of the Royal Savoy Association shall be the assistance of men in the said Home or Homes for short holidays by the provision of travelling expenses and expenses of accommodation and maintenance at the said Home or Homes or elsewhere.

In the Schedule accompanying the Scheme was set out the '2 acres, or thereabouts, together with the messuage erected thereon formally known as "The Gables" ', the adjoining land 'containing 2 roods 38 perches … together with the messuage erected thereon known as 'The Elms' and land in Brougham Road 'containing 10 perches or thereabouts, together with the cottage erected thereon'.

Thus was the legal basis established and the funds and activities of the two charities fused into a unity. The First President was Her Majesty The Queen and the First Vice-President Lady Juliet Duff. The Governors were drawn from both charities and were: Mrs. Hay, Miss Dorothy Yorke, Sir Francis Fladgate, Stanley Bond, William Oates, The Duke of Richmond and Gordon, Cecil Chapman, Sir Alexander Hood and Cecil Knox.

(It was not until September 1995 that all reference to The Royal Savoy Association was removed from the constitution. It would, however, be difficult to over-estimate the importance of that fund in establishing the ethos of Gifford House in Worthing and that institution's capability to measure up to the high ideals of Lady Ripon's vision.)

Meanwhile, the day-to-day detail of actioning the purchase was going ahead—with the occasional hiccup; Mrs. Coccioletti took away all the keys of 'The Gables' by mistake and, when she returned them, had to take one off the ring 'which she thought was the key of their own strong room in London'! Mrs. Hay did ask Patchings to give their opinion on the combined value of the two properties but, in a letter to her, they did not quote an actual sum but contented themselves with comparative generalities:

> It is very possible that for some big development scheme, such as a Private Hotel, Nursing Home, School etc. the value of the two properties is very much enhanced. A site such as this in the heart of the pre-war developed area is certain to considerably appreciate in value as the town grows, and this is now assured owing to the advantage of the electrification of the Southern Railway.

Their fixation with the railway is striking, their indulgence in split infinitives less so!

On 4 March 1933 the first turf was cut by the Mayor of Worthing, Councillor T.E. Hawkins. By May, the Governors were unhappy about the lack of progress on the work needed to the buildings. Tenders had been invited and the contract was awarded to The Ashford Builders Company of Bloomsbury Park, London, who had submitted the lowest bid and of whom the Mayor of Worthing was the chief partner; labour was to be drawn from the unemployed in Worthing. But progress was not satisfactory. Mrs. Hay, writing to Mr. Oates, complains that she had

> another 'rough and tumble' with Mr. Bruty of the builders—who is so impossible to deal with, to my mind … Mr. Bruty had the audacity to tell me that if I would listen to him instead of to you and Mr. Morgan it would be much better—in other words, he can take me in but he cannot take in you and Mr. Morgan! I have made up my mind not to be worried, but to go straight ahead.

A site meeting was held in April 1933 to ensure that everything possible was done to speed up the work. Although there had been some modifications to the original plans, there was nothing which invalidated the agreement on the date of completion in the contract time of 16 weeks, and Sir Francis wrote to the architect asking for his guarantee on prompt completion.

Electricity was adopted as the cooking medium, for by so doing the Worthing Corporation would grant a special rate of ⅝d. per unit plus £4 2s. per kilowatt as well as instal new mains at no cost to the home.

It was decided to name the Hospital 'Gifford House' and this would be painted on the gate-posts at the main entrance, while a bronze plate would be fixed on the front door bearing the names of the Queen Alexandra Hospital Home and the Royal Savoy Association. The Governors also 'inherited' the gardener and odd-job man at 'The Gables', Mr. G.P. Casey. He had served his apprenticeship at Granard and at Ripon House; Mrs. Hay commented on 'how small the world is' and added that Casey 'is an Irishman and rather "whiney", but I think he is quite a good gardener'. She re-engaged him, raising his wage by 15s. a week to £2 15s., and he agreed to find his own accommodation in the town. Mrs. Hay lost no time in telling him exactly which plants were to be moved and where, and which were to be left strictly alone!

Mrs. Hay's copies of her correspondence, still held on file in Gifford House, reveal the scope of her control and the variety of activities with which she had to deal. Not surprisingly she received many letters from prospective employees, of whom a good number were ex-service-men. Some had been wounded in action but were able to work, others had not been able to find any regular employment since discharge. One letter from a Worthing address ran: 'I am applying for the Situation as General "Handy-man" of the "Gables", Worthing. I have had experiences with Central-Heating, Electrical maintenance and General Cleaning, I am an ex-Naval man having served 22 years, Rank on leaving the Royal Navy, Leading Seaman, Leading Torpedo Man. An interview to suit your convince would oblidge [*sic*]'. Mrs. Hay's reply was a model of courtesy and kindness, as it was when a married man applied for a position as an orderly: 'I am sorry that we have no post to offer you … We have a large staff here and are unable to take them all and also our orderlies have to be unmarried men who live in'. But when she was able to help, she did as in the case of George Knapper, who lived in Tunstall, Stoke-on-Trent. Knapper's brother seems to have contacted Mrs. Hay in the first instance, and she was able to offer this unemployed man a position with the builders as soon as the building began. His letter of appreciation, one page long and all one sentence, was most moving. When his local Labour Exchange raised some bar to his taking up the post, Mrs. Hay wrote to them, and sent Knapper 20s. for his fare to Worthing and assured him that he could have a room over the garage, 'with fire and light provided' at 35s. per week and that Casey 'would feed you and do your washing for 18s. a week'.

One employee whom Mrs. Hay recognised for his efforts during the planning of the move was the workshops officer, Bob Morgan. He had done much to make the planning as smooth as possible and had spent much time in Worthing with the builders, paying attention to the little details which turn into major disasters if they are not attended to. At the end of June 1933 Mrs.

Hay was happy to tell him that the Finance Committee had voted him a salary of £300 per year on his move to Worthing in the same post and added:

> I wish to take this opportunity of thanking you for the very valuable work that you have done for our men here and for the good of the Home, during the past twelve years, and to tell you how delighted we are that you are coming with us to Worthing.

He came—and he continued to serve with loyalty for many more years.

We have been paying a lot of attention to grand schemes and negotiations, so perhaps a dip into more prosaic detail will be a useful antidote, and it does throw an interesting light on the finances of the day. For example, the insurance premium for the building for the first year was—£11 15s.! The Ministry of Pensions allowed 10ft. per bed space, and so it was possible to plan for 42 beds with an option to fit in a few more if necessary at a later date. The wards, the temporary buildings, were to be built on the most sunny side of the house, as the Matron agreed with Mrs. Hay that the recreation room could face north as it was not essential to have a good outlook, the men only being in there for meals, for games on a wet day, or in the evenings. In total, the additional buildings required were:

1 recreation room
2 or 3 wards with WC's, bath rooms, sluices and sinks
2 small single rooms for ill patients
1 small sitting room for the Sisters
1 ward kitchen

and kitchen accommodation with scullery, larders and stores. For the floor covering, Mrs. Hay corresponded with Ernest A. Barrett, Builder, Cabinet Maker and Funeral Furnisher in Angel Lane, Hayes End, who wrote to her in a large, scrawling hand showing detailed measurements for each room. Eventually, an order was placed for 600 sq yards of 'first grade Greenwich linoleum' at a cost of £127 19s. 6d. George Brettle & Co. wished to quote for much of the material needed for curtains etc.; in a rare typing error, Mrs. Hay had to return a 'beadspread' which the 'Chairman did not approve of'. She jibbed at a quote of £1 2s. 6d. for each new electric point, which Mr. Morgan thought to be too high.

Matters electrical generated a fair amount of correspondence, and sometimes she had to be diplomatic. In dealing with the General Electric Co. Ltd. of Kingsway, London Mrs. Hay had asked for and received a quotation but it was not one that she was able to accept as 'another member of our Committee really had this matter in hand … He has now chosen some other fittings which, I agree, are not nearly as nice as yours, but he thinks they will suit our requirements and with our shortage of funds it is necessary for us to keep our expenses as low as possible'. In writing to the Electricity Department of the Borough of Worthing, who were responsible for the supply, she wrote: 'In the matter of the expense of the laying of this cable, I earnestly beg that you will be as lenient as is possible with us, remembering the cause for which we are starting this Home—i.e. for totally disabled ex-service men'. The company responded with an offer to lay the cable for a nominal charge of £5. Then into more technical detail; feeling concerned about the capacity of the cable, she pointed out that 'we shall have only about four horse-power in driving motors' but that the load would increase as soon as the workshops were opened. Finally, there was the estimate provided by the Electricity Department for the total cost for one year: £206 11s. 5d. The cost of the entire refrigerating plant and cold store amounted to only £170 12s. 6d. Then there was the question of the hard water of Worthing, and Mrs. Hay quoted 'an old gentleman living next door [Mr. Sams!] … and he has lived in Worthing all his life … and has never had a water softener [because] he never allows the water in his house to be more than 120° and therefore gets no trouble with corroded pipes'. She had some concern because in the small electric boiler used for making the tea there was 'a thick sediment at the bottom every day and also a white layer over the top of the water of a chalky substance'. She fired off a broadside to the supplier of paint to the builders because their Alpha preparation was far too expensive and she was 'horrified' at the extra expense; a week later she received a credit note.

We finish this episode in the history of Gifford House with a last look back at the Roehampton building and there is a sadness in the air. A sale of surplus equipment was arranged through A.W. Taylor & Co. of Putney, to take place on Tuesday 5 September 1933. Mrs. Hay stipulated that any posters about the auction were not to be displayed until only a day or two beforehand as Mr. Charrington did not want to see them there. Mrs. Hay had visited the home for the last time on Thursday 17 August to hand over the keys. She recalled that it was a sad occasion and Mr. Charrington could not face saying farewell to them.

The final issue of the *Gifford Journal*, the 55th, focused on the memories of the previous 14 years—on the comrades who had passed on, many of them 'shining examples of courage in making the best of life, and getting the most out of it under the handicap of disablement', and on the many friends and supporters who had brought so much life and happiness into the patients' lives. They had said farewell to the much-loved Regent Telephone girls when the exchange was converted to automatic dialling and the staff dispersed, but a farewell party was a great success and the girls were invested with 'The Gifford Order of Good Fellowship' as a mark of gratitude. This was also awarded to many people who had given their support over the years, for example to Miss White 'our Salvation Army Lassie' who used to 'come along with her mysterious little bags of bulls eyes and cough drops—the blessings that have been poured upon those little bags she will never know'. Benefactors, whether families or individuals, were thanked but none more so than Mr. and Mrs. Charrington whose house they had been able to call 'home' for so long. Mrs. Hay added her own tribute, for their generosity had been wonderfully good— and words were inadequate to express their heartfelt thanks. She ended her letter: 'On behalf of my "boys" the Committee—Matron— and myself, I thank you all most gratefully, and full of HOPE for the future happiness of our New Home'.

CHAPTER 9

♦

WELCOME TO WORTHING

And so the move to new pastures took place, not without expressions of regret from local people and not least the Wandsworth *Borough News*. An editorial, reminiscing about the 14 years in which disabled soldiers had been cared for, maintained that the fine old mansion would long be remembered for 'the stricken but cheery good fellows who paid so heavily in the war, the countless people who rendered voluntary service to bring bright hours into their lives, the officials and workers and the great-hearted man [Mr. Charrington] who made all this possible by lending this palatial residence at a time when such a place was urgently needed'. (No private resident ever lived in the house again. During the Second World War the house and grounds were used for training purposes. The house then stood derelict until the early 1950s when it was demolished to make way for the LCC Ashburton Estate. The site of the house is roughly where Tildesley Road joins Putney Heath.) Mrs. Hay wrote to the paper thanking its readers and everyone who had supported the Home over the years and hoping that the comparative nearness of Worthing might be a cause for contacts to be maintained. She added that, thanks to the kindness of Mr. Cearns of the Wimbledon Greyhound Stadium, the majority of the patients would be travelling to Worthing in their chairs in the Greyhound vans, and for this the Wimbledon Branch of the 'Lest-We-Forget' Association and its chairman, Mr. William Oates, would be assisting.

And so the first convoy of the 35 pantechnicon-loads of furniture and equipment set out on 31 July 1933, the final delivery being completed 10 days later. The contractor was Elys of Wimbledon who quoted £4 16s. 0d. per load, each of 600 cubic feet. The patients came in five convoys over 9 and 10 August.

The *Worthing Herald*, under an article titled 'The "Boys" Are Arriving', described how they were met by Mrs. Hay and Miss E.A. Luce who, in her capacity as secretary to Mrs. Barrington-Mudd(Commandant of the Worthing branch of the Red Cross Society), had been taking an active interest in the home since its preparations began. The paper noted that the mother of one of the patients, E.L. Holland, lived in Goring. Mr. Holland had been forced to lie on his back for 12 years but was now able to walk after two and a half years' treatment in Switzerland. The reporter approved of the three newly-constructed wards, the sun verandahs and the three smaller wards in the house. The feature of the day room was the billiard table which the patients had insisted on bringing down from Roehampton. (The removers for this were Jelks & Sons of the Holloway Road who charged £8 10s. including its re-erection.) Another reporter, following up this visit in October, was amazed by the response to his question, 'How do you like Worthing?', for in each case the response was a hearty 'We like it!'. He was particularly impressed by a patient who had lost both arms and legs and who demonstrated his ability to extract a match from a box and light a cigarette 'with hardly more fumbling than a man with the use of both hands'. The only major difficulty he encountered was when Mrs. Hay complained that very few houses and places of entertainment had doors wide enough to take wheelchairs, and the ban on such chairs in the cinemas was a hard aspect for the men to bear. Apparently, the ban was due to Council regulations, but the manager of the Odeon vowed to have the problem solved; in the meantime, a local man was taking in his portable cinema

45   *The Day Room, Worthing with billiard table*

to Gifford House. In the following May, the Matron was able to report that the three cinemas had made special arrangements for wheelchairs to be admitted, free, to the afternoon performances; the local Theatre admitted walking patients and staff free for the weekly matinees; Brighton and Hove Albion also admitted patients free of charge. She had earlier commented on the 'very kind reception' from the people of Worthing, their many offers of entertainment (amounting to one concert per week), parties and lending cars for drives. A warm welcome came from the Worthing Rotary Club whose Chairman, Mr. A.G. Linfield, would play such a prominent part in the life of the Home for four decades. The Worthing Red Cross detachment was giving voluntary help in the wards and a ladies' sewing party was tackling the linen which needed mending. Also of great help was the way in which the Red Cross ferried patients between London stations and Victoria, and the co-operation of the Worthing police in lending their ambulance to collect patients from the station. And, not surprisingly, it was not long before the men found the sea to be a real attraction, even to fishing from the pier; on one occasion, the Worthing Sea Angling Association organised a competition for them.

The formal welcome from the town came on 31 October when the mayor, Councillor T. Ernest Hawkins, held an 'At Home' at Gifford House. The guests included the Duke and Duchess of Richmond and Gordon, the Dowager Countess of Leitrim, Lady Juliet Duff and Miss Dorothy Yorke, Lady-in-Waiting to the Princess Royal (and also a governor). Every part of the home was open to the guests. Mrs. Hay took the opportunity to mention the £4,000 debt on the buildings, that there was insufficient finance to build the second of their sunrooms, an aviary was needed for the homing pigeons and until a workshop could be built the men were having to take an enforced holiday from their pastimes. Her appeal did not fall on deaf ears, for the response of the people of Worthing both immediately and in the longer term showed that they appreciated the situation. (In November 1936, Mrs. Hay was able to report that there were 6,000 names on the list of the supporters of Gifford House.) It would be tedious to list all the contributions which were to be made, but some examples will suffice. A collection at the interval in the Plaza cinema made £5 (multiply by 30 for today's values), the Essex Lodge Bridge drive raised £15 5s., an anonymous donor treated 22 patients to a coach drive and tea at Bramber, the Worthing Working Men's Club sent gifts from their harvest festival, as did Parham Church; the Worthing Hockey Club donated the proceeds from the sale of programmes at their Easter festival; a dance was held at the Plaza ballroom on an August Bank Holiday Monday and dancing recitals at the Pier Pavilion by the pupils of Miss D. H. Muirhead and Miss M. McBirney both gave the proceeds to Gifford House. Perhaps one of the most attention-catching was the meeting chaired by Mrs. Hay in which Grey Owl held the attention of 2,000 people at two separate two-hour sittings in the Pier Pavilion. The son of a Scots father and an Indian mother, and married to a Mohawk Indian, he fascinated the audience by the story of his total change from being a trapper (especially of beaver) in Canada to someone who was determined to protect all species of wild animal in that country. His was a spell-binding talk, illustrated with film and was the first in a tour arranged by Ramsdens Bookshop of 11, Chapel Road. And although today's activities are usually less dramatic, the steady flow of contributions into Gifford House from local groups and societies, as well as from absent friends, indicates that local people still have the Home's interests in mind. Our story will now have to move on and in so doing focus on the larger fund-raising efforts, but the reader should not forget the quiet, undemonstrative support which is so important to the Home. Indeed, the staff and Governors can well echo the words of Mrs. Hay's letter of thanks at the end of the first year at Worthing: 'We have had much to be thankful for during our first year at Worthing. We have made many good friends and to them as to our old loyal friends who have so generously helped us—and without whom we could never have achieved our object of carrying on this Hospital Home—we offer our most sincere and heartfelt thanks'.

One unexpectedly sour note does emerge from all the fund-raising activities. Apparently, some person or persons were calling on Worthing residents soliciting donations on behalf of Gifford House, and Mrs. Hay had to make a plea in the local press saying that such activities were quite unauthorised and any information should be passed to herself or the police.

In February 1934 a new chapel was dedicated where, as the *Worthing Gazette* reported, 'A Stable One [*sic*] Stood'. Mrs. Hay wished it to be referred to as the 'Chapel of Remembrance'. The building had originally held loose boxes for horses, and this fact provided a golden opportunity for the Archdeacon of Chichester, the Ven. B.G. Hoskyns, to draw an analogy with the stable at Bethlehem. The congregation included Lady Juliet Duff, the Duke and Duchess of Richmond and Gordon, the Mayor and Mayoress (Alderman H.T. Duffield and Mrs. Duffield) together with patients in their wheelchairs. A memorial tablet was unveiled by the Rector of Heene, Revd. E.A. Haviland. The Archdeacon dedicated the building 'To the glory of God and to the sacred memory of our first President, Her Majesty Queen Alexandra, and Gladys Marchioness of Ripon, in whose memory the Home was founded, and to all our old comrades of the War who have passed on'. The names of these 'Boys' were entered in a Book of Remembrance which was placed in a niche in the wall. (This book remains in the chapel and the tradition has been maintained.) Boys from Heene Church choir led the singing of hymns, which included 'We love the place, O God' and 'O Valiant Hearts'. The service ended with the singing of the National Anthem.

The highlight of 1934 was undoubtedly the visit of the Duchess of York on 23 May. Her association with Gifford House had begun with visits to Roehampton in 1928 and 1932, and still continues in her role as President today. Dubbed the 'Smiling Duchess' by the local press,

46   *The Duchess of York receiving a posy from patient J. Telfer*

excitement was generated in the town. She came at the invitation of Mrs. Hay and agreed to receive purses on behalf of the Home. A League of Helpers of Gifford House had been formed to support its activities and fund raising. Its Chairman, Capt. H.C. Bowles, wrote in the local press that it had been necessary to fix the minimum amount for a personal presentation for each purse at £5. 5s. although smaller contributions would be gratefully received. Owing to limited accommodation, admission to the garden party would be by invitation only, but the Home would be open to inspection later and the Committee wanted to 'cordially invite the inhabitants to inspect the Home'.

The 'inhabitants' turned out in force for the visit and the grounds were full to capacity in what was one of the largest garden parties ever held in the town. The streets of the town were decorated with bunting but the time of Her Royal Highness' arrival had been kept secret. In fact, she had arrived some time before the function was due to begin and she was inside the gates of the house before many people had arrived with the expectation of seeing her. She was then escorted on a private tour of the building (much to the chagrin of the press who called the reason for their exclusion 'inscrutable'). Her tour of the house exceeded the hour planned, due to her interest in the wards and in meeting the patients. Apparently she commented on the light, airy nature of the wards and on the attractive colour scheme. She took the opportunity to buy several toys for the young princesses before planting two trees to commemorate her visit, both being taken from the Duke of Richmond's estates, one at Goodwood, the other at Gordon Castle in Scotland. So, slightly later than planned, the Royal visitor and her party made their way to the platform on the lawn, where nearly a thousand people were waiting.

A lady reporter of the *Sussex Daily News* described the Duchess' dress thus:

> Gowned in a lovely creation of powder blue crêpe-de-Chine, a cleverly modelled frock and three-quarter length coat to match, her Royal Highness wore a blue picture hat trimmed with daisies.

Presumably the delay in sighting this creation only served to heighten the reporter's excitement!

One of the patients, J. Telfer, in his wheelchair, made a presentation of a posy of lilies of the valley to the Duchess. Before receiving the purses, a telegram from the Queen was read by Mrs. Hay:

> I am very pleased to know that the Duchess of York is receiving purses today for the new home for disabled soldiers at Worthing. I hope the soldiers may be comfortable and happy in their new surroundings, and I send my warmest good wishes to them, and to all connected with Gifford House. Mary R.

In the absence of the Duke of Richmond through illness, Lord Leconfield, the Lord Lieutenant, welcomed the Duchess to Worthing. He praised the work which Mrs. Hay had given to the Home and, mentioning the debt of £4,000, hoped that the purses would go a long way to paying it off.

Her Royal Highness then received purses from associations and individuals representing many aspects of Worthing society together with some from Wimbledon and also national groups.

47 *The Duchess plants a tree to mark her visit. To her left are Mr. W. Cheal (whose nursery supplied the tree), Mr. Algernon Hay, Mr. Stanley Bond (governor), Mr. William Oates, Mrs. Hay, Lady Juliet Duff and Miss Fletcher, Matron.*

Speaking on behalf of the Home, Sir William Goschen announced that the purses which had been presented totalled £1,060 13s. 6d. which included £242 1s. 6d. from absent friends. A further subscription of £446 10s. from friends in Worthing brought the total for the afternoon to £1,507 3s. 6d. A little while later the Duchess left for Goodwood House, by which time the neighbouring streets were filling up with spectators. People lined the road all along the front, South Street and Chapel Road. The *Worthing Herald* reported that 'Her Royal Highness passed, bowing and smiling to the right and left. A few moments and the Duchess had passed out of sight. There was no cheering. Sussex people do not raise their voices in public, not even for a Royal visit'! But the Band of the Royal Sussex Regiment played on in the Home, as they had during the whole event, bringing to the end a colourful and memorable visit by the 'Smiling Duchess'.

(One further comment upon a little detail. The reporting of the names of those attending took up two full columns in the *Herald* which, finding itself having to re-plan its layout, expressed its debt to three clients who had agreed to the removal of their advertisements to another page— Patching & Co., Searles, and the British Union of Fascists—the last of which had contributed a purse on the day.)

Fund-raising took on a national flavour when, in May 1935, the BBC granted an appeal to Gifford House in the 'Week's Good Cause'. The appeal was made by Revd W.H. Elliott, vicar of St Michael's Church, Chester Square, a friend of Mrs. Hay and well-known for his regular Thursday evening broadcasts. A Worthing resident recalled that he was at school in Sussex with Mr. Elliott, who was nicknamed 'Bones' by his fellow pupils. Whatever the aptness of that nickname, 'Bones's' appeal raised the princely sum of £4,230 within a fortnight. Gifts were received from 'all over the British Isles and from English people living on the continent. We have just signed the 5,164th receipt', purred Mrs. Hay; there were over 2,000 anonymous donations, and two of £100.

A fund-raising venture of a quite different nature was arranged by Lady Juliet Duff. She decided to hold a Dinner to celebrate the Silver Jubilee of the accession of King George V. Together with Lord Westmorland, she gave an 'At Home' at 3, Belgrave Square in December 1934. The *Worthing Gazette* reported that the first planning meeting 'took the very pleasant form of a cocktail party, at which, I imagine, quite as much, if not more, useful business was done and enthusiasm aroused, than at a more formal gathering'. The Ball eventually took place at Claridge's on 7 May the following year; dinner was at 9pm and dancing at 10.30pm. For the gastronomically curious reader, here is the menu for that august occasion:

> Melon de Jersey
> Coupe Prince de Galles
> Filet de Sole Monseigneur
> Poularde de Bresse Maryland
> Laitue Effeuillée
> Biscuit Glacé Gismonda
> Quartiers de Comice Caprice
> Friandises
> Moka

And the wines? Niersteiner, 1925; Corton Bressandes, 1919; Pommery & Greno, 1926; Kopke's, 1927 and, finally, Hennessy's ('over 20 years old').

The *Sunday Times* published these vignettes:

> Lady Juliet Duff, a charmingly restrained chairwoman, typifying the national rejoicings by wearing a white dress with a cloak of dark blue tulle and carrying a red pochette. Canon Sheppard a very secular figure in the most immaculate of evening dress clothes. A very witty and apt speech by Mr. Duff Cooper.

It must have been a brilliant assembly judging by the guest list (including a certain Mr. and Mrs. Laurence Olivier). The result of the evening was that £2,000 was donated.

Sadly, on that same day, Gifford House lost a very good friend and benefactor, the Duke of Richmond and Gordon. A descendant of Charles II, he showed a remarkable courage throughout his life, not least in managing his estates of more than a quarter of a million acres with very limited inherited resources. Ill health during his youth limited his ambitions regarding a military career but he did serve as ADC to Lord Roberts in Ireland and South Africa, where he was awarded the DSO. On the formation of the Irish Guards, he obtained a commission and retired with the rank of major. At the outbreak of the Great War he was in command of the Sussex Yeomanry. On the eve of leading his regiment to the front, he was struck down by an attack of spinal meningitis which brought on partial paralysis. He had to rely on the support of crutches or a wheelchair, and no doubt this enabled him fully to understand the feelings of the Giffites. He was remembered by many as the friend of crippled soldiers and as an ideal employer.

His funeral, at Boxgrove, was attended by a distinguished gathering, and Mrs. Hay with four patients represented Gifford House. The guard of honour at the church was made up of employees, members of the Royal Sussex Regiment and the District Scouts. The cortège made its way to the Brighton crematorium but diverted at Worthing to pass in front of Gifford House where the

patients were drawn up in line to say their farewell to one whose interest in them was so great. In accordance with the Duke's wishes, instead of flowers, friends were asked to send donations to Gifford House, a charity in which he had been so interested. One of the patients, Mr. F. Dawson, wrote this tribute to the Duke:

> To the 'boys' at Gifford House the Duke was a true and loyal friend. He was himself seriously disabled, and often, when paying us a welcome visit, might have been seen along with one or two patients, propelling himself round the grounds in his invalid chair. Ever since the end of the War he took the keenest interest in our welfare, and I think it is no secret among us that, had it not been for his initiative and the ever-ready help he gave to our chairman, Mrs. Algernon Hay, CBE, the new Gifford House at Worthing would never have come into being.
>
> The Duke himself was no mere 'figurehead'. He was a real friend to all of us 'boys'. Only a few weeks ago the duchess motored him over to see us, and although he was then unable to leave his car, he asked for many of us by name to draw alongside for a few words of greeting. We little thought that would be the last time he would

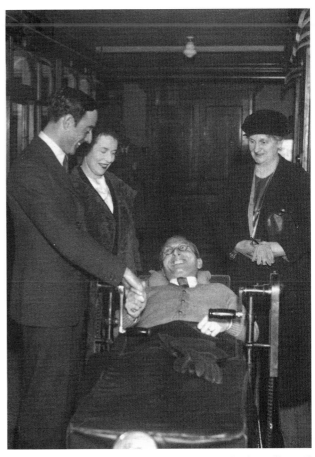

48   *The 9th Duke of Richmond and Gordon, with the Duchess, talking with Pensioner Kelf and Mrs. Hay*

be among us, and we are proud and grateful to know that he was thinking of us right up to the end.

The Duke's son, the 9th Duke, took over his father's offices of vice-chairman and joint honorary treasurer. He visited Gifford House several times informally after his father's death, but made his first official visit, with the Duchess, for the second day of the annual sale on 14 December 1935. Mrs. Hay, in her welcome, said that they were honoured by his having come there that day; the Duke's direct response was: 'Honour be blowed; it is entirely my privilege to be able to come here'. His father had taken such an interest in the Home, and that had been the reason for his 'very quick acceptance of the opportunity to carry on that work, and perhaps add a little bit, too'. He did indeed keep a lively interest and later was to be Joint Honorary Treasurer. His son, the 10th Duke, is still a Patron. A Sun Shelter, paid for from the Floral Tribute Fund for the 8th Duke, was opened by the Bishop of Lewes on 13 June 1936, the ceremony being combined with a garden party and a sale of handicrafts. The shelter proved to be a popular acquisition especially when, despite the sun, there was a cold wind blowing (Worthing is not dubbed 'windy' for nothing!).

This is probably a good point at which to take stock of the patient situation, or else we shall be ignoring the most important people in the home. Who were they, how did the Governors manage to care for them, and, the other side of the coin, how did they care for the staff who were so vital a part of the total care programme?

When the patients came to Worthing, they were in three distinct categories as far as funding was concerned. The highest number were funded by the Ministry of Pensions, and these patients were referred to as 'Pensioner'. Another group was funded by the Joint War Finance Committee and the rest funded by the Governors. At the beginning of 1934, out of the 49 beds available, 33 were funded by the Ministry, two by the Committee and six by Gifford House, with two holiday patients and six empty beds. The Ministry number declined very gradually but five years later was still running at 25. The last Joint War Finance Committee patient left in May 1935 and the number funded by the Governors had risen to 13 in 1939, when holiday patients were occupying 11 beds. The holiday patients numbered 94 in 1935, rising to 115, 125 and 150 in the succeeding years. The question of finance throughout these years was always determined by the source of funding.

At the end of 1934 there were 40 permanent patients and this is how they were classified for treatment, all being the direct consequence of war service:

Paraplegia following gun-shot wound of spine	11
Gun-shot wound of head and complications	5
Disseminated sclerosis	3
Post-encephalitis	3
Miscellaneous diseases of the central nervous system	6
Multiple arthritis	6
Bronchitis and asthma	1
Thrombo-angeitis obliterans	3
Miscellaneous	2

The Medical Superintendent, Dr. Oliver Gotch, was able to state that from a medical standpoint the move to Worthing had 'been a definite move for the better. The absence of fog (except for a slight sea mist now and then) compared with London conditions has been a great gain'; he was convinced that, had they remained in London, the prevailing fog conditions would have added to the death roll. He was also enthusiastic about the Vita Glass which had been installed in the Sun Rooms, and the consensus of medical opinion was that it provided a positive benefit and would soon be universal in all hospitals. (Dr. Gotch gave long service to Gifford House, finally retiring in 1959. He was a considerable artist and musician and had a great interest in the Classics; one of his charming foibles was to refer to members of the staff by classical nicknames which he had chosen for them!)

Let us look at some of the ways in which permanent cases were handled; examples of particular patients illustrate the situation vividly. The Governors received a request to take a patient named A. Swingler who was admitted on the understanding that he should pay the home a proportion of his pension towards the cost of his maintenance. The sum agreed was 25s. per week. From this there developed the further understanding that he, together with any other patient admitted permanently, should undertake to return home for one month in July or August in order to leave the bed available for holiday 'visitors'.

One patient, Pensioner Auger, quoted by Mrs. Hay in one of her reports, was a veteran of the Afghan and South African Wars as well as the Great War. His wife had died and he had lived on his own for some years, in some sadness. General More, hearing of his situation, arranged for him to be admitted to Gifford House. Mrs. Hay said: 'He is now 76. Auger has been welcomed by all our men. They already call him "Daddy", and I hear him giving great accounts of his past life'. Another patient with a compassionate need was Pensioner Skinner from Carlisle. With his right arm amputated at the socket and injuries to both legs, he had been cared for by his mother but she, now aged 80, was unable to look after him. Skinner was very grateful to find a haven in Gifford House.

A more troubled course of entry fell to Pensioner E.A. Pink, a patient at Queen Mary's Hospital, Roehampton. His Old Comrades Association had nominated him but Mrs. Hay had to tell them that the Ministry would be most unlikely to agree. Sir Lisle Webb agreed to take up the matter with the Ministry, but it was an Admiral Sueter who successfully persuaded them to pay for his admission as a holiday patient for six weeks. After 15 months of discussion, he was admitted as a permanent patient paid for by the Ministry of Pensions at a capitation rate of 11s. per day.

A former patient, Stocking, had been a head case at the King George Hospital at the time when Matron had been on its staff. Dr. Gotch, who had examined him from time to time, thought that a holiday at Worthing might be very beneficial to him, and that was subsequently arranged.

These instances give a flavour of the kinds of decisions facing the Governors. In another instance, a patient recommended by the Sunderland Branch of the British Legion was admitted for a course of treatment and permitted to stay for a further month. Another was financed to the extent of two guineas per week by the Emergency Help Committee so that he could receive treatment for his chronic bronchitis. One patient, G. White, admitted through the auspices of the Surbiton Branch of the 'Lest-We-Forget' Association, suffered from chronic syringomyelia and was helpless from the neck downwards. He had no-one to care for him at home when his sister was away, and a successful application was made for him to be admitted as a Ministry of Pensions case.

But some wanted to leave! In February 1938, for example, Pensioner A.A. Holl, who had been a Ministry patient at the home since 1920, applied for his discharge—to get married.

One final item. In 1939 there was living at the home John Jervis, the son of a former patient. He was described as 'of weak intellect' and did odd jobs around the home. The Governors discussed his situation and had to ask his father to remove him to Graylingwell (Chichester). We must give the Governors credit for sensitive handling of people issues in some very difficult circumstances.

One of the more vexing aspects of patient care concerned the funding of treatment which was not available at Gifford House. For example, Pensioner J. Telfer required teeth extractions and a complete set of dentures and had received an estimate for £7 5s. The Governors established the rule that each case should be considered on its merits and in this instance decided to grant 25s. towards the cost of treatment should it exceed the estimate. Mrs. Hay then applied successfully for a grant from the Prudential Approved Societies. There was special feeling for Telfer because he was the senior patient in the hospital, having been with them since the day he had been brought home wounded from Arras, on the Somme, on 22 March 1918. He it was who had presented the bouquet to the Duchess of York on her first visit, and when he eventually died in March 1936, aged only 39, Dr Gotch felt that he could claim that the 'extraordinary good condition of Telfer for so long a period [was due to] the splendid male nursing'. 'Jerry', as he was known, had enlisted in the Northumberland Fusiliers at the age of 17. His commanding officer, Colonel Shakespeare, continued to take an interest in his welfare and wrote to Mrs. Hay paying tribute to Telfer's 'grit and bravery' during his long years of suffering and thanking the hospital staff for its 'kindly and loving care' of him. Mrs. Hay later received a letter from the Chief Area Officer of the Ministry of Pensions in Newcastle expressing his grateful thanks for 'the valuable assistance the Home had given in the case of Pensioner Telfer'. Welcome compliments, no doubt gratefully received.

Other external treatment had to be provided. Pensioner L.J. Collins had to be sent to St Thomas' Hospital for a special eye operation, and the Governors agreed to pay the hospital 5s. a day for his maintenance. Several patients received grants for dental treatment, ranging from £1 5s. to £3 3s. 6d. Contributions were also made for the purchase of spectacles although, where optical treatment was necessary due to pensionable disability, application to the Ministry was made. One less usual treatment was that of Pensioner J.W. Anderson who was admitted to the Royal Mineral Water Hospital in Bath. The Compassionate Fund was used to pay for this at 28s. weekly.

As had to be expected, there was the inevitable sadness as some patients died. Frank Dawson, who died on 13 January 1939, had been one of the first paraplegic cases, having been admitted to the King George Hospital on 1 June 1916 after receiving spinal wounds whilst serving in France with the Yorkshire and Lancashire Regiment. He had originally been a Ministry patient and been discharged from Gifford House in 1926 but re-admitted four years later as a hospital liability patient. This gentleman was the first editor of the *Gifford Journal* to whom we owe so much contemporary information about the home at Roehampton. He it was who wrote the verses for the Christmas cards which were sent out each year; they were modestly initialled 'F.D.' It is a hope that this volume will be an albeit inadequate tribute to his memory by the recording of some of his many writings.

It is instructive to note that Dr. Gotch had, by the end of the period under review, to remind the Governors that many of the patients sent by the Ministry of Pensions were classed as 'derelict' cases and that the death roll would be heavier than usual. Such are the demographic realities of life and death.

One other instance is worth noting. Following the death of George Smith in 1937, Mrs. Hay reported that she had received a letter from his widow in which she stated that the Ministry of Pensions did not regard her as eligible for a pension. The Governors agreed to take this up and to ensure that the matter was placed before her local branch of the British Legion. Just one of the countless instances when that sterling body was approached to investigate and correct the interpretation of rules which, owing to their necessarily global nature, needed to be reviewed for individual inconsistencies.

A slight diversion at this stage. In the minute book of the House Committee, there was a regular entry for 'Renewals', viz. for any items of expenditure for which the Matron had to get approval. The range of articles is wide and some of the costs revealing. For example, she was permitted to purchase a new infra red radiation lamp for £9 17s. 6d. 'less the usual discount', a piece of flannelette for making up into bed jackets, a mincing machine for 22s. 6d. and a potato peeling machine for £5 from Harrods. The Ronuk polishers were re-bristled (new they cost 25s.); 500 yards of cretonne was bought for curtains and screens, and there were almost monthly requisitions for crockery, brooms, baking tins and other impedimenta. Clothing was a regular feature and one entry was for '3doz large vests for patients—also socks—3prs extra large pants for one patient'!

To return to the question of finance. We have seen how critical was the need to establish a source of funding for each patient and that the bulk were funded by the Ministry of Pensions. It is hardly surprising, therefore, that the Governors spent much of their time either arguing or defending their case with the Ministry. The Ministry held considerable sway in these matters even, for example, in the question of granting leave to 'their' patients at Gifford House. The Governors would report these movements and the fact that the patients had all returned as planned. The Ministry worked on the calendar year for leave entitlement, but this caused some difficulties. For example, Pensioner Kelf who arrived at Gifford House in the middle of a year had accumulated only 10 days' entitlement by 31 December, but patients were not allowed to take less than 14 days' holiday at any one time. This kind of problem was taken up by Sir Lisle Webb for resolution, but far more demanding of time and energy were the debates about funding.

At the beginning of 1934, the average cost of patient maintenance was 13s. per day. Whereas the Joint War Finance Committee (who admittedly had very few patients) would fund at the actual rate, the Ministry did so on a more discriminatory system. We find, for example, at one time Pensioner Rust being funded at 7s. but Pensioner Isaac at 11s. per day, this latter being the maximum amount. The difference had always to be met from Gifford House funds and, as these were necessarily limited and were themselves non-guaranteeable as far as frequency and amount of contributions were concerned, the balance to be struck was often extremely fine. There was also the thorny question of the re-admission of patients who had previously been discharged but who, for a variety of reasons, wished to be re-admitted. The Governors held a year-long correspondence with the Ministry on this topic alone, with Lady Juliet Duff paying personal calls on the Minister himself and the Governors continuing to set out their case in comprehensive letters. One of the unusual aspects of these negotiations was that the Minister was asked to become a patron.

On the medical scene, further argumentation ensued with the Ministry in the case of Pensioner J.S. Hewer who was transferred from Queen Mary's Hospital, Roehampton on 4 September 1939. His eligibility for a disablement pension was his arthritis but he was found to be suffering from pulmonary tuberculosis. This was reported to the Sussex Medical Officer of Health but there were no available beds in the county. Queen Mary's Hospital also had no room to take him back and, anyway, T.B. was not the patient's pensionable disability! The law ruled that once the County Medical Officer had been notified, the patient could not be moved and he therefore had to stay at Gifford House (which was totally unsuited to handle such cases). Sir Lisle Webb again agreed to take up the cudgels with the Ministry, asking them to take the case or to get Hewer transferred. A Dr. Templeton visited and agreed to get in touch with the patient's home town of Gloucester. A thoroughly non-committal letter came from the Ministry and once again Sir Lisle went to see Colonel Moore. Finally, on 9 January, Hewer was moved to the Isolation Hospital at Swandean.

The benefit to holiday patients was considerable. This is well illustrated by the case of Mr. Henry Jeremiah May who had served for 12 years in the Royal Engineers before being wounded in the War. He was given, on discharge, a 50 per cent pension of 25s. a week for himself and his wife. Unable to walk, he remained at home, a four-roomed flat in East Greenwich, with a typical London outlook. His rent was 9s. a week and although his sons gave him 7s. 6d. a week he could never consider having a holiday. So he would remain for 12 months on end in his room unless a son was able to take him out. When his plight came to the notice of the British Red Cross, they arranged to finance a month's stay in Gifford House. His rapture was reported by the *Worthing Gazette*:

> It's a grand thing to be welcomed in so a lovely place like this. Everyone here is magnificent—
> Matron, sisters, nurses, orderlies. They make no fuss about rules and regulations—behave
> yourself and do practically as you please is the regime. I have been taking medicine three
> times a day for six or seven years; today the doctor said I could knock it off.

The paper then adds rather poignantly: 'In the flat at East Greenwich is Mrs. May. The last holiday she had was nine years ago—a day at Margate'.

These events should not be regarded as purely derogatory of the Ministry of Pensions or to criticise bureaucracy in a pejorative sense. Rather, they illustrate the situation which will always face those who care for the sick or disabled: who is to care, and who is to pay? The budgets will never meet the total need and governing bodies will always find themselves in conflict with whatever organisation holds the overall purse-strings. It is clear, however, that the Governors were persistent in their advocacy and on that alone should be congratulated.

Let us now look at how they organised and managed the staffing of Gifford House. During this period, there were between 35 and 39 staff on the payroll, including a few part-time staff to care for up to 50 patients. The rates of pay inevitably catch the eye. A masseur was engaged at £2 2s. per week, a male nurse at 45s. rising to 60s. and a trained night duty nurse for £65 pa. A new orderly was engaged at 25s. per week—and one already on the staff had his pay brought up to that amount from 21s. After one year's service, the rate was increased to 28s. This was also the rate for the porter. By the end of 1936, the orderlies' rate was raised to 35s. according to length of service; a nurse's salary was £52 pa. One orderly, who had 9 years' service, was permitted to work with the male nurses, under their supervision, especially for lifting patients, and for this received £2 per week. It is perhaps instructive to note that Dr. Gotch was receiving a salary of £45 16s. 8d. per month and the Matron £22 13s. 8d.

One of the most significant ways in which the Governors were able to help their staff, and in which they showed great understanding, was on the question of sick pay. This is well illustrated by the case of Nurse Reed who entered St Thomas' Hospital on 1 March 1939 for an operation. She was entitled to sick benefit of 12s. per week, her salary was £43 pa. The Governors decided that, in view of her nine years' service, they would make up the difference while she was under treatment and convalescing. Similarly, when Nurse Mercer was ill and had to return to Scotland, her full salary was paid and also her full return train fare; she also had nine years' service. When Sister Murrell fractured her hip while on duty in April 1937, she was taken for treatment to St Thomas' Hospital. Application was made to the Sun Insurance Company who agreed to pay 30s. a week, the maximum sum allowable under legislation. The Governors wrote to the Chairman of Sun Insurance— Sir William Goschen!—asking for a hospital grant to be paid; they would make up her full salary. Sister Murrell came out of hospital on 16 July and went to the Normanton Nursing Home at a specially-negotiated rate of three guineas per week. Later, following a satisfactory X-ray, she went to a convalescent home at Hunstanton; the support which she received from the Governors must have been a great relief to her.

One situation was not so conveniently resolved. On 3 December 1938 the under-gardener, Bob Bright, was run into by a car. The Governors agreed to pay his wages although the matter of the National Health Insurance was not resolved, pending assessment for accountability for damages by the driver. Bright's solicitors eventually obtained an ex-gratia payment from the insurance company for £30, and gave him a cheque for £27 18s., deducting two guineas for expenses. Bright had, however, signed for £30. The Governors consulted their solicitor, Mr. F.G. Stevens, and decided that he should be paid the full £30. However, as he was now in receipt of an old age pension, and was unable to work, they reluctantly decided to dispense with his services.

These are but a selection of instances of the ways in which the Governors acted at the personal level, and they will be judged well by posterity. It is a truism that no organisation is better than its employees, and that has its positive evidence in the record of Gifford House over the years, and any governing body will ignore its chief asset at its peril. Now we must return to more weighty matters.

Another Royal visit occurred in 1937, when the visitors were Prince and Princess Chichibu, the prince being the brother of the Emperor of Japan. Their visit, on 21 April, was private and lasted about an hour; they were staying in Hove at the time in preparation for the forthcoming Coronation. Both were fluent in English and were particularly pleased to meet Sgt. Hair and 'Bobby'

Brown who had both served in Japan. In Ward 3 they found the Japanese flag displayed alongside the Union Jack; they did not know of the extraordinary efforts which one of the patients, George Pickerell, had had to make in order to find a flag. He had scoured the town in vain, and then, despite placing an order for one to be made, the flag did not arrive on time; a last-minute combing of the town produced one in the nick of time. The Royal guests were especially interested in the workshops and also in knowing how many such homes there were in England; Mrs. Hay replied that there were several but Gifford House was the only one which took patients for holidays.

49   *The Crown Prince Chichibu of Japan and the Princess talking to Pensioner A. Stoker*

In 1938 was held the first Garden Fête. The object was not to make money but, as the Committee minutes put it, 'keep up interest in the home and to get more sales for the men's work'. No invitations were sent out but an advertisement inserted in the local press. There would be an admission charge of 1s. and in one of the unnumbered programmes would be a number which would enable the winner to claim a prize donated by Queen Mary. (The lucky winner turned out to be a Mrs. Harmes of Richmond Road who became the proud owner of a Chinese tea caddy.)

The date for the Garden party was 23 July 1938, from 2 to 7pm. and it was opened by Mr. Christopher Stone, known colloquially as 'the prince of radio beggars' due to his popularity as a broadcaster and his very successful charitable appeals on the radio; he had himself served in the Great War (MC, DSO) and lived at Wiston. Nearly 1,800 programmes were sold though the attendance was about half that number. Mrs. Hay was able to tell them about some typical patients' cases and also to extol the benefits of the holiday scheme. Sir William Goschen took the opportunity to explain the financial situation. Although they were able to fill their beds over and over again, there was a very tight funding situation. They received capitation grants for 25 out of the 40 cases, which meant having to raise £6,000 each year from their own resources. He mentioned, too, that they were acquiring 'The Elms', an adjoining property which would be used as a nurses' home.

The Round Table were responsible for organising the sideshows, and the West Chiltington Silver Band gave their services free. (When discussing buffet teas, it was decided that, rather than hire crockery, it would be better to 'purchase a gross of cups and saucers from Woolworths'. The teas were sold by ticket at 1s. 6d.)

Another Royal visit occurred in the following year, when the Princess Royal visited the town on 21 June to open the new children's ward at Worthing Hospital. She then lunched with Mr. and Mrs. Hay at their home in Lansdowne Road before visiting Gifford House, where she was welcomed by the Lord Lieutenant, Lord Leconfield. Her Royal Highness toured the home, paying particular interest in Mr. E. Wholey, a patient for whom she had been instrumental in finding a place at Gifford House. She planted a silver birch tree and then received purses totalling £259.

Our chapter has to end on a sad note. From November 1939, one significant name does not appear in the minutes of the Combined House and Finance Committee—that of Mrs. Hay. The cause for her absence was illness, and she had had treatment for cancer as far back as 1936. But this illness gradually took its toll, and she died on Saturday 27 April 1940. Born in 1875, 25 years of her life had been devoted to the work of caring for disabled ex-servicemen. She had gone to the help of Lady Ripon at the King George Hospital, in the running of the Compassionate Fund and Gift Stores, and was given Lady Ripon's place as President at her death in 1917. She worked there daily until it closed in May 1919 and inaugurated the Home at Roehampton. In addition to her interest in Gifford House, she helped the Joint Council of the Order of St John and the British Red Cross Society with the 'Hospital Ward Industries', on two occasions being asked by them to make a tour of the hospitals in England on their behalf. She was also in charge of the Hospital Ward Industries stall at the Imperial Institute Armistice Exhibition for several years. She was a member of the Committee of Queen Mary's (Roehampton) Limbless Welfare Fund. She was awarded the CBE in 1924.

The Queen sent a telegram to Mr. Hay: 'Your loss will also be deeply felt by all those disabled ex-servicemen to whom Mrs. Hay devoted the last 25 years of her life. I join with them in gratitude and appreciation of her great works'. Mr. and Mrs. Hay had made their home at Chester Lodge in Worthing (long since demolished and a block of flats built with that name). In addition to her work for Gifford House, she was a governor of the Star and Garter Home at Richmond, a vice-president of the Horsham and Worthing Division of the British Red Cross and a member of the Committee of the 'Lest-We-Forget' Association and the Lynmouth Welfare Committee. The *Worthing Gazette* headed its obituary, 'Funeral of Founder of Gifford House'. A private service was held in the chapel, conducted by her nephew, Revd. Maitland Bald, assisted by the Chaplain, Revd. H. Hancock. The service was relayed throughout the home, and a guard of honour of patients and staff watched as the funeral procession moved out of the grounds and made its way to the crematorium at Brighton. At the same time, a memorial service was held in Heene Church, conducted by the rector, Revd. E.A. Haviland, and attended by representatives from many of the charities with which she had been associated.

Lady Juliet Duff penned this moving tribute to Mrs. Hay:

> The Hospital Home was her conception, and since its opening in 1919, she devoted her entire life to it, and her first and only thought was for the welfare of the men she loved so dearly and understood so well.
>
> Their uncomplaining heroism was, I know, a help and an inspiration to her in facing her own troubles; two severe illnesses, one a few years ago, and this last illness, which was to end so tragically, had sapped her strength but had left no mark on her indomitable spirit, and through them both her thoughts were never of herself, but always of the men to whose service she dedicated her whole being.
>
> Until the evening before her death, though desperately weak, and often in pain, she carried on from her bed the business of Gifford House; it was to the very last, her only preoccupation. We who are left to carry on her great work must, and will, see to it that our men lack for nothing that was theirs during her lifetime; to do this we shall need your help more than ever. We earnestly beg you to help us in our work for Mrs. Hay's 'boys', who alike in their suffering and in service for their King and Country, have given us such a shining example of courage.

A memorial window to Mrs. Hay, designed by Lilian Peacock, was completed and placed in the chapel. The window depicts healing miracles from the four gospels.

Let the last words be from Mrs. Hay's own lips. Speaking at the Annual General Meeting in 1936, describing some of the activities of Gifford House, and the kind of help which was being given to patients, she said: 'Our motto is "Never say no, when it is possible to say yes" '; that is the most fitting epitaph for a remarkable and gifted lady.

CHAPTER 10

◆

THE WAR YEARS

As the shadows of impending conflict loomed over the nation in 1939, it was inevitable that the Governors should review the role of Gifford House and its facilities. By March, in correspondence with Dr. Hebb of the Ministry of Health, they offered to the Ministry 40 beds to be placed at its disposal, pointing out that the Charity Commission Scheme only permitted admission of men who had served in HM Forces. They felt that their priority should still be to those men who had suffered in the Great War and suggested two categories of patients whom they should take:

> 1. ex-servicemen from the Great War who were in Ministry of Pensions hospitals which were in danger zones, and

> 2. those paralysed and seriously disabled ex-servicemen living at home in danger zones and who had been visiting Gifford House under the holiday scheme.

The wisdom of the Governors in the first suggestion lay in the fact that such patients would, *ipso facto*, be paid for by the Ministry, thus reducing the burden on the Governors' funds. There was a proposal to convert the workshops to wards but this was abandoned, for it was realised that the workshops were more important than ever to keep the men employed and motivated. So two extra beds were put into each ward and the upstairs staff wing was converted into wards, and a total of 22 extra beds were provided, bringing the capacity to 73 beds. (The construction of temporary buildings for wards had been contemplated but was not followed through as planning permission would not be forthcoming.) An appeal to the Joint War Finance Committee resulted in a handsome grant of £500 to equip the extra beds. In fact, the Ministry of Pensions took up the Governors' offer and transferred 12 of their patients from St Mary's, Roehampton (together with their capitation entitlement). The remaining beds were soon filled with the other category suggested by the Governors. The implications are seen by a typical breakdown of the types of patients; in 1943, there were 32 Ministry of Pensions cases whom they funded, 12 for whose maintenance Gifford House was totally responsible, and 16 patients admitted for the duration of the war, their homes having been damaged by enemy action, whose maintenance was entirely dependent on voluntary contributions. All this meant that the holiday scheme had to be abandoned; a limited resumption was made in the following year when some patients admitted from danger areas had to return home for various domestic reasons. Not surprisingly, there was a high bed occupancy throughout the war. A further restricting factor was that in view of the transport difficulties and the rationing restrictions, the Ministry of Pensions stopped granting leave to the permanent patients, thus reducing the opportunities for short-stay holiday occupation. In 1941 the Ministry did ask if paraplegic women and children could be accommodated but it was pointed out to them that the constitution specified only ex-servicemen as patients, a slightly ironic *volte face* from the position in the Great War when the King George Hospital sought assistance from the North Staffordshire Infirmary (see p.7).

The question of the evacuation of the patients in an emergency had to be tackled. After communicating with the War Office and the Regional Commissioner of the Ministry of Home Security, the Governors were told by the Ministry of Information that military occupation of the

50 *The Princess Royal outside the workshops, June 1939*

Home was unlikely, and it was therefore decided to take no further action. The Petroleum Board advised that, in the event of any evacuation, petrol would be supplied by the Police. The Police referred this to the Town Hall and the Town Clerk subsequently wrote to Miss Fletcher, the Matron, stating that arrangements were being made for 'the computation of a census of invalid persons'. A WVS visitor called to obtain the information. The Town Clerk told the Home that if evacuation did become necessary, infirm persons would be removed by ambulance train rather than by road. However, contingency plans were made for evacuation should unexploded bombs fall nearby and the patients were to be moved to the nearby St Botolph's schools or the Church Assembly Rooms in Heene Road.

In 1941 some thought was given to moving the patients to an empty house on the outskirts of the town as a kind of 'shadow accommodation' but the Ministry of Works and Buildings advised against such action. (The number of ministries involved seems endless!) Again in the summer of 1942 the same question was raised by Mr. Linfield, at that time a governor, and who was to play a significant role as Chairman. His adhesion to this topic is clearly revealed in the minutes of the Governors' meetings. After reviewing the previous correspondence, it was decided to write to the Director General Medical Services at the Ministry of Pensions. The concern was about the acceptance of liability for the removal of the Ministry patients should the need arise and Mr. Linfield contacted the Regional Medical Officer of Health about the non-Ministry patients. The former replied by a telegram laudable for its brevity: 'If and when necessary agree transfer of S Pensioners to Ministry Hospital probably Roehampton. Signed Prideaux'. In the meantime, Lady Juliet Duff had been in touch with Sir Phillip Chetwode of the Red Cross who could not offer any alternative accommodation. Nor when she met the Minister of Health, Mr. Ernest Brown, did she make any progress; he explained that owing to the lack of accommodation, the compulsory evacuation scheme for coastal areas did not involve the removal of institutions catering for chronic cases, and such institutions should continue to function in those areas. He thought that Worthing was unlikely to be affected as it was not a port. Mr. Linfield received a reply in the same vein, and contacted the Worthing police and the Town Clerk to put them in the picture.

Meanwhile, the Matron had spoken to each of the patients individually. Apart from one or two who wanted to consult their families, all the patients stated that they preferred to remain in Worthing with the Home and to be looked after by the staff who understood them, rather than be transferred to other hospitals. Miss Fletcher also spoke to the staff who, except for one or two of the daily staff who had young children, were willing to remain in the hospital in the event of the compulsory evacuation of the town. In the light of experience of the war in Worthing, all this activity may seem to have been somewhat frenetic, but one only has to consider what the effect might have been of a bomb falling nearby to see that this contingency planning was sensible.

The other activities associated with the war were not unfamiliar to any family in Worthing. The difficulties in blacking out the Home were considerable in view of the number of windows and doors and their unusual and non-standard sizes. The police requirements in this respect were precise and there was a heavy expenditure to be met for the blackout material. Some commodities became scarce; Miss Fletcher was authorised to build up her stocks of soap owing to increasing prices and she purchased two years' supply of material for the nurses' uniforms. She also purchased six regulation steel helmets at 12s. 6d. each to be used by the orderlies on A.R.P. (air-raid precautions) duty. Gas masks were provided for the male orderlies—after representations to the Ministry of Pensions who authorised the supply of three civilian gas respirators. The contents of the hospital were insured against war damage for £10,000; a revaluation on 1943 raised this to £12,000. The Governors did consider building a concrete shelter but, after Mrs. Hay discussed this with the patients, they decided that they would much rather remain in their beds during an air raid. The Warden was Mr. Bob Morgan who had worked so hard in preparing for the move to Worthing, but his home was 20 minutes away from the hospital and contingency plans were made with the Head Warden of Group 2 of the A.R.P., Mr. Leadbetter. A night watchman was engaged for A.R.P. duties at a wage of £3 per week; Mr. Morgan attended a special course for 'Roof Spotters' and trained up the other house wardens. All this met with the approval of Mr. Leadbetter who had advised the action to be taken. In order to guarantee fuel supplies, new petrol tanks were installed with a capacity of 3,000 gallons, about one month's supply, the cost being around £125. A new gas steamer costing £49 was bought as insurance against the breakdown of the electricity supply. Perhaps the only gain from the rationing was reflected in the accounts for 1942, for the cost of provisions, especially butter, bacon, eggs and meat had decreased considerably.

The provision of drugs was, of course, vital and Dr. Gotch initiated the purchase of a stock of necessary items. Prices had begun to rise, caused partly by the introduction of purchase tax and partly by the fact that many supplies, which originally came from what were now enemy or occupied countries, were now difficult to obtain. Foreseeing a possible shortage, he wanted to lay in a supply which would be sufficient for three or four years. An order was placed with the suppliers, Duncan and Flockhart, and the initial supply of drugs and dressings, which was to suffice for about two years, was ordered at a cost of £82 10s. 10d. The supplier agreed to hold the stock in the warehouse, at no charge provided that the cash payment was made with the order. This was done, and when the supplier later revealed that no insurance was carried on it, the Governors took out War Cover insurance of the stock at 5s. per cent. One innovation had been made just before the outbreak of war. In July 1939, Mrs. Hay had questioned whether it would be desirable to have an internal telephone system installed. The Committee thought that it was a necessity and Mr. Oates offered to make inquiries of firms who had experience of such systems (he mentioned the Austin Motor Co. in Birmingham). Mrs. Hay said that a representative from Dictograph was visiting three days later; one is not surprised to discover that a new system was subsequently installed within two months, at a cost of £176. One marvels at how they had been able to function without such a system.

The situation regarding the patients can be seen from some of the reports which Dr. Gotch made to the Governors. In June 1941 he commented upon the sharp increase in the number of deaths of patients, describing the figures somewhat lugubriously as an 'outstanding feature' of the past six months. However, he analysed the figures and pointed out two determining aspects. First, many of the fatal cases had been in hospital for many years, some as many as 20 years, suffering from grave illness and disabilities from war injuries; it was inevitable that such a mortality rate should

51 *The Memorial Window to Mrs. Hay in the chapel*

occur. Second, half the number of deaths were from those admitted from danger zones and who were in the final stages of illness, e.g. cancer, heart disease and disseminated sclerosis. But the treatment for the patients was still being administered at the pre-war standards and he praised the nursing staff for their devotion to their duties. The Worthing hospital also was praised for their valuable help in cases requiring emergency treatment of a surgical nature, sometimes including staff. Members of local Red Cross detachments gave literally thousands of hours voluntarily to the hospital. Further, some of the convalescent patients had freely offered their services; their willingness to lend a hand was, he felt, also a benefit to them in helping them to cope with their disabilities. There were times when, due to fuel shortages and severe winter weather, the patients were acutely uncomfortable though no serious outbreaks of intercurrent illness occurred. The upstairs wards continued to be used for walking cases (as was the practice in Roehampton) and at the end of the war, when some patients returned to their homes in London, these were the wards with vacant beds. There was, however, one significant outcome concerning the mix of patients. The beds had been occupied by cases from the Great War, and except when an occasional vacancy occurred, no cases from the present war could be admitted. Dr. Gotch concluded his report:

> During the late European War, the abnormal conditions then prevailing obliged us to take as many of these helpless cases as we could reasonably nurse, and treat, but we now feel it imperative that no further vacant beds should be so filled. I understand that the British Legion are considering opening a special hospital near Bournemouth for the advanced type of helpless cases. When this is ready to receive such cases, it will prove an inestimable boon to these unfortunate sufferers and meet a very pressing problem for all concerned, particularly with respect to Gifford House, whose main function in the past has been the care and treatment of cases with some potentiality towards recovery. It is obvious, too, that occupational therapy, as given by our workshops, can play no part in a completely helpless case. Handicraft instruction of some kind is an essential feature of treatment to all cases other than the helpless and we are aiming at a re-establishment of our workshops to full working capacity as soon as the material, such as leather, wood, cane etc. becomes available in normal quantity.

This was how the workshops were described at about this time:

> The Work Studios, fitted with benches especially adapted to the men's individual disabilities, are a hive of industry, where you may find them happily engaged in such varied handicrafts

52   *Gifford House at the beginning of the war. The wards are seen top left. 'The Elms' is on the right and behind it are the coach house and chapel.*

as:- soft toys, pewter work, hand-woven bags, feather mounts, caning of chairs, baskets, rugs and beadwork etc. The men take a real joy in their work, and of course only do it as and when they feel able. When too ill to go to their Workshops, they may often be found working in their beds. As one of the paralysed men once wittingly said: This is a great place for Handicaps and Handicrafts.

The first Christmas of the war saw all the patients (except for two whose homes were in Worthing) 'confined to barracks'. This was because the Ministry of Pensions cancelled all home passes owing to the transport difficulties. To the relief of the Governors, no doubt, the Joint Council of the Order of St John and the British Red Cross Society made their usual Christmas grant of 5s. per head; hopefully, this enabled an element of festive cheer to be experienced in the Home. The restriction on leave applied during the following year and must have been a considerable frustration to all. However, for these patients, it was arranged to pay from the Compassionate Fund the travel expenses of wives who would otherwise have been unable to afford to travel (not being restricted themselves as civilians). This cost the Compassionate Fund about £12 a year, and must have been a most welcome gesture.

Writing over 50 years later, the daughter of a patient recalled the atmosphere of the time. Mrs. May Cheesman, whose father was William Impey, used to visit him with her mother. They had to apply for a permit to travel 'and could not go through the railway station without it. That permit was like a piece of gold'. She remembers Miss Fletcher, 'such a wonderful lady always coming to see us when my mother and I visited'. Her father called Gifford House his 'Paradise'; he had been collected from their home in East London to stay for the duration of the war. She recalls that her father 'always seemed to be invited everywhere' and how ladies would come to Gifford House and 'escort the patients to the beach and then arrange tea in their homes'. Mr. Impey's best friend was Mr. Swingler whom we met in the last chapter, and photographs taken at the time depict some very happy faces. Mrs. Cheesman still has in her possession some of the jewellery which was made in the workshops—a reminder of the value which crafts played in rehabilitation.

The Governors were less fortunate when *they* sought assistance. They asked the Ministry of Pensions to pay constant attendance allowance for four patients who had been admitted since the beginning of the war but they received a very firm response to the effect that the allowance could not be paid to pensioners in institutions. Fortunately this did not deter them from their long-standing attitude of compassion and understanding, and their wish to say 'yes' if at all possible, for both patients and staff. For example, they were able to give the holiday patients pocket money of 5s. or 2s. 6d. a week depending on circumstances. In early 1943, Dr. Gotch was authorised to 'purchase one dozen half-bottles of champagne at 26s. a bottle' for the patients; in May 1944 each Ministry patient received 35 duty-free cigarettes per week paid for by the Ministry and the British Red Cross; the Governors paid from the Compassionate Fund for the same number to be provided for the 14 patients who were hospital liability. In that same year, Christmas gifts and stockings were sent by the British and American staff of the Mission for Economic Affairs and War Shipping Administration at the American Embassy in London. It is good to read that, when the Director General Medical Services, Ministry of Pensions, Dr. Haward, visited the hospital on 3 September 1943, he confessed his great satisfaction with all that was being done.

Not everything was all sweetness and light, however. One of the difficulties with holiday patients was, as Dr. Gotch pointed out, that from a distance the staff had only a brief medical report written on the application form, leading to a certain amount of risk in accepting them. A tragic example was the regrettable mistake made by St Bartholomew's Hospital (later fully acknowledged by them) of sending a Mr. H.F. Whitta who was discovered to be suffering from cancer of the stomach and in a terminal state. The man, clearly not a case for treatment, died at Gifford House but Dr. Gotch commented that at least the nursing staff had the satisfaction of knowing that his last days were made as comfortable as possible.

On a completely different aspect, Dr. Gotch reported in May 1940 that Pensioner F.G. Brown was in arrears with his weekly payment of £1 towards his maintenance and 'had been behaving in a manner contrary to the Rules of the Home'. A letter of apology was received from Brown who promised to resume payment within three weeks and to make up the arrears. It was decided that Sir Lisle Webb and Dr. Gotch should interview him and take 'such steps as were necessary'. Within three months, Brown wrote a letter to the Governors thanking them for all the benefits he had received and asking for discharge as he had obtained employment whilst away on a fortnight's leave. But by November, the Ministry of Pensions informed Dr. Gotch that Brown's health had broken down; the reply was that he would only be re-admitted if the Ministry accepted financial responsibility for him; Brown was eventually admitted to St Mary's, Roehampton.

In July 1940, Mr. Algernon Hay (who was heavily involved in the Home) reported that he had been in touch with Brig. General More of the United Services Fund about the recent bad conduct of Pensioner Coleman, who was subsequently told that, if he caused any further trouble in the hospital, he would be dismissed without warning and the police informed. And when, in September 1943 the Ministry requested the admission of one Christopher Copson, who had been admitted twice previously, they were told that this would not be possible as Copson was 'an exceedingly troublesome man'.

But there were patients whom the Governors would have dearly liked to admit but were unable to do so for lack of space. The Ministry asked them to admit two patients with disseminated sclerosis, but the Governors had to reply that they already had their 'full quota of this distressing type of case' and could not admit any more for the present (March 1944). A similar situation had occurred the previous year. Two applications had been received from the British Legion and the Joint Council Emergency Help Committee. Again, Dr. Gotch had to point out that they had their full quota of 'helpless cases, which require extra nursing and also make the outlook very depressing for those patients who can get about'. One of the nominees was totally paralysed and was not admitted; the other could stand and walk a little and was admitted when the holiday patients had gone home. This was in some contrast to the patient who died in September 1944 of the debilitating effects of a form of neurosyphilis.

In January 1943 Dr. Gotch seems to have been surprised by the application for discharge by Pensioner W. L. Barker, injured in the present war and a complete paraplegic. Barker wished to get married but Dr. Gotch considered him to be unfit for discharge since he required further treatment. The Ministry agreed with Dr. Gotch but Barker was adamant and the Committee wrote to him to say that they disapproved of his decision, but that did not stop him from taking his discharge on 20 February 1943.

What of the nursing staff in the war years? In May 1939 Mrs. Hay had begun her report at the annual meeting thus:

> The work of the hospital goes on much the same, and I think very happily, since there is really a very happy atmosphere in the whole place, and I think it is very much due to our very wonderful Matron and the staff. The letters that I get from 90% of the men who come for a holiday, not one of them ever leave out the kindness and motherliness of our Matron, and how it really is Home from home. I do not think we can ever realise how much we have to thank the Matron and all the old staff. We have got 5 Sisters who have been with us since 1919 and 3 since 1915 [one hopes they understood her use of 'old'!]

The praise of Miss Fletcher and the staff was to be a regular feature of the meetings of the House and Finance Committee throughout these years.

At about this time, the total salary bill for one month was £151 16s. 6d. with State insurance costing £8 19s. 8d. (Over 50 years later, and with a staff which had doubled in size, the monthly cost was around £100,000.) Four years later, in accordance with the recommendation of the British Hospitals Association, it was decided to adopt the Rushcliffe Report Scale of salaries for the nursing staff, even though this added £500 during its first year, though the Government were willing to pay half the extra cost. There was a distinct preference for resident nurses, not least because the Governors felt them to be more economical to engage. Where it was necessary to engage non-resident nurses, they were employed at the same daily rates as nurses at the Red Cross Convalescent Homes and Auxiliary Hospitals, i.e. £1 2s. 6d. plus £1 1s. 0d. board and lodging. Deductions were made for partial board:

Breakfast	3s. 3d.	a week
Midday dinner	7s. 0d.	" "
Tea	2s. 6d.	" "
Supper	3s. 3d.	" "

A war bonus of 5s. per week was paid to Charman, the chauffeur and Casey, the gardener. Later, the latter was to develop pulmonary tuberculosis and his wages were paid for some months during his illness. He was himself an ex-serviceman and had, by 1944, more than ten years' service at Gifford House. When he became too ill to work, he was given one week's notice, a gratuity of a further fortnight's pay and his pay made up in full for three months. His successor was engaged at a wage of £4 5s. 0d. per week. (This was a year after the Matron's salary had been increased to £325pa and Dr. Gotch's to £600.)

One item which gave the Governors serious food for thought was their wish to introduce some kind of superannuation scheme for the staff (today, something which is taken for granted). The initial investigation was undertaken by the accountant, Miss Knowles (the first woman ever to qualify as an FCA). She verified that about 75 per cent of the staff would be eligible to join and the annual

53   *Matron Fletcher at her desk*

cost to the hospital would be about £440. Sir William Goschen and Mr. Wright of the Joint Council were in favour of the Scheme and, after approving it in principle, Miss Knowles went ahead and it was inaugurated by December, rather grandly named the 'Federated Superannuation Scheme for Nurses and Hospital Officers (Contributory)'. For those staff who were not eligible to join, an amount corresponding to 10 per cent of their current salaries, plus emoluments, was transferred to the Nurses' Compassionate Fund as a provision for their retirement allowances. For those staff who would have received entitlement had they throughout their service contributed to the Federated Superannuation Scheme, and the Pension of Civil Servants, it was decided to grant a pension of £52 per annum for 20 years' service, or a corresponding amount according to the number of years they had been on the staff.

The Governors continued to pursue their policy of sensitive handling of personnel issues. Nurse Gray, who had 20 years' service, was given six months leave of absence to return home to look after her aged mother for a time. Two Sisters, who did not come under the Rushcliffe Scale because they were not State Registered, were nevertheless awarded the full salary increase which would otherwise have been due to them, the Hospital bearing the cost. Sister Hulbert, who spent many additional hours contributing to the efficient work of the office, was recognised by payment of honoraria. Sister Ryall, who left shortly before the end of the war after many years with Gifford House, was awarded a leaving present of £50 in addition to her pension. Similar thoughtfulness was shown when Sister Murrell, after long and devoted service, expressed the wish to retire. And the death of Sister Warner on 29 April 1945, after having joined the Hospital in 1919, brought from the Governors a glowing appreciation of her service. But the lady who deserved so much recognition was duly recognised. Miss Fletcher, who had remained in Gifford House during every night of the war, and who had so effectively run the hospital during those testing years, was awarded the MBE, and in May 1945 the Governors minuted that 'it was particularly requested that Matron should take a month's holiday this summer, now that the War is over'.

How were the financial affairs of Gifford House faring? One of the yardsticks was the cost per day of patient care. The House and Finance Committee report for November 1940 showed that the average cost per patient for the first nine months of the year was 11s. 4d. (57p) compared with 11s. 10d. for 1939 and 13s. 5d. for 1938.

> This reduction does not mean that our high standard for food and Hospital treatment has been in the least affected. It is due to our increased numbers and to constant vigilance on the part of those responsible for the management and buying.

In 1942 the cost had risen to 12s. 3d., and 13s. for 1943, and that was accounted for by a decrease in the number of patients. (In the same year, the cost of provisions was 1s. 5½d. per day.) In 1944 the average cost rose to a very precise 14s. 3·65d. and, as that was only 1s. above the 1938 figure, the financial controls on costs can be judged to have been very successful. Some of the savings seem quite startling. For instance, Miss Knowles reported in December 1943 that a saving of 8,000 gallons in fuel oil had been achieved in comparison with the pre-war period; electricity consumption was down by 10,000 units per annum and 500,000 gallons of water had been saved. All this in the face of a doubling of prices for many items since the beginning of the war. Early in 1944, Miss Fletcher reported that the tailor who had made the patients' suits for many years had gone out of business and that she was experiencing great difficulty in finding a new supplier. The Committee agreed that Utility Suits would not meet the patients' requirements owing to their various disabilities and Matron was authorised to make the best arrangements she could in the circumstances; six months later she requisitioned a new sewing machine for £21 5s. 11d.

The income of the home, not unsurprisingly, continued to exercise the minds of the Governors. The basic problem was that there was an operating deficit, as these figures show:

	Total Expenditure	Total Income	Deficit
1941	£14,077	£10,979	£3,098
1942	£14,060	£10,762	£3,297
1943	£15,011	£11,497	£3,513
1944	£17,303	£13,068	£4,235
1945	£17,773	£14,400	£3,373

The covering of these deficits depended upon charitable and other donations. A major source was from charities who gave regularly during these years, foremost being the Joint War Finance Committee whose custom it became to give two donations in most years towards reducing this deficit. Their payments were in tranches of £500 or £1,000 and they also responded with a cheque for £500 when the number of beds was increased and emergency equipment was needed. Other major donors were the British Legion Benevolent Fund, the United Services Fund, the War Charities Collection Ceylon, and the Alexandra Rose Day Committee. Grants were also given by the Smith's Charity Kensington Estate, the Queen's Hospital Facial Care Committee and Courtauld's Ltd. But throughout this time, one of the most encouraging factors must have been the flow of legacies, often from local people and nearly always in memory of someone in their family who had had some contact with the armed forces—over 90 per cent of the legacies were from the estates of women. On the matter of Covenants, there was far greater benefit to be received than today. As was pointed out in the promotional material with the annual reports, 'for each guinea paid by the subscriber, the Hospital can receive a further guinea from the Inland Revenue', the covenant having a period of at least seven years.

A major source of income was from the BBC Radio Appeals in the Week's Good Cause. Mention has already been made of Mr. Christopher Stone and his interest in Gifford House. His appeal on 9 March 1941 was a joint one with the Star and Garter Home, Richmond and St David's Home, Ealing. Unfortunately, owing to an air raid warning being in operation on that night, the appeal was not heard by the majority of listeners in the south. The BBC arranged for a second appeal in September, Mr. Stone again speaking on behalf of the three homes. Over 9,000 letters were received in response to these two appeals, and the share for each home was £2,113, an overwhelming result, not just in financial terms but in knowing that, in spite of the straitened circumstances of many in the war years, those who had fought for their country were not forgotten. A further appeal was broadcast on 3 January 1943; the beneficiaries were the same, but Lieut. Esmond Knight was the broadcaster (many will remember him as the television and cinema actor who refused to let his blindness restrict his activities). His appeal was stirring and each charity this time received £4,000. In February of the following year, Sqn. Ldr. John Strachey made the appeal and each charity received £1,550. Gp. Capt. Douglas Bader made the appeal in June 1945 and the splendid amount of £7,700 was credited to each charity. One should note that these appeals were a shared effort, each charity accepting the organisational responsibility in turn; the administrative workload was immense and the Governors expressed their gratitude to the staff whose 'hard work and long hours' had all been carried out 'without a hitch'. They also expressed their thanks to the Post Office Retired Officers Association for their assistance and the Westfield Secretarial College, Worthing for the help which they gave.

During these years, life was lived as normally as possible within the constraints laid down by the wartime conditions, and this was especially true of the social life of the hospital. The most difficult times for the patients were the long winter evenings when the blackout restrictions were a necessary but unwelcome restraint on social activities. A series of games competitions were devised to pass away the hours and whist drives were one feature, often organised by friends of Gifford House. Gifts to the patients at Christmas were a great tonic and, where possible, outside trips were arranged. The Garden Party concept was shelved for obvious reasons nor were the patients able to take part in the usual sale and exhibition at the Lord Roberts Workshops in London. But thanks to the support of the Brighton, Hove and Worthing Gas Company, the Christmas Sale was held in their showroom in Chapel Road, Worthing from 9 to 14 December 1940. Matron's call to the residents of Worthing was in these words:

> It is very essential that we should find an outlet for the men's hobbies, which give them an added interest in life, as well as benefitting [sic] them financially, and a successful sale is always a great encouragement to them. We are hoping that the residents of Worthing will patronise the men more especially this year, since owing to war-time conditions, we were unable to hold our garden fete this summer and therefore the patients are relying upon the success of the Christmas sale in order to dispose of the handicrafts they have made during the past year. I would again stress the fact that all the proceeds of this sale go to the men themselves.

The result was that the proceeds totalled £92 2s. 5d. which was considered extremely satisfactory and far in excess of expectations. This event proved popular each year; in 1944, for example, 1,230 articles were put on sale, and nearly all were sold. And in the following year, the men made thousands of poppies for Remembrance Day so there was no lack of activity on their part. They also helped to raise money on Alexandra Rose Day each year, their self-propelling chairs becoming a familiar sight around the town centre and nearby roads. In the late summer of 1940, as their contribution to the Worthing Spitfire Fund, the sum of £30 10s. 10d. was sent to the Mayor, having been raised by the sale of lucky tickets and donations from the staff.

On 4 June 1940 a successful outing was made to the races at Lewes. Visiting groups and personalities to Gifford House were always welcomed, and the list is a very long one! Here are a few to illustrate. In July 1939 'Rubber Face' Fred Gwyn, the 'crown prince of comedians', appearing at the Pier Pavilion, dropped in to give the men his own hilarious display of facial contortions. On a more serious note, in November the Worthing Boys' choir gave a concert of many popular airs, including 'The Bells of St Mary's'. Local artists gave a concert on Boxing Day and the Clough Studio of Music and Drama kept up their tradition of an annual concert. In November 1940 the Picardo school of dancing performed various 'turns' and their tap dancing was apparently much appreciated; these were followed by choruses and songs, all under the direction of Miss Bunty Morgan. Miss Jessie Thomas, LRAM and her Selden Studio of Music gave a 2½-hour concert in May 1941. In July, there was a splendid outing to Thakeham for a strawberry tea at the nurseries of Mr. Linfield; many patients were driven there by members of Worthing Rotary Club and those in

54   *Ward 1*

wheelchairs went by lorry. And so the list could continue … a record of sterling support by the residents of Worthing and charitable associations, noteworthy among these being the 'Not Forgotten' Association and the 'Lest-We-Forget' Association.

Behind much of this activity was Mr. Arthur Linfield. He had, in his capacity as Chairman of Worthing Rotary Club, given a warm and supportive welcome to Mrs. Hay and her 'boys' on their arrival in Worthing in 1933. The Rotary Club and the Round Table were to remain most loyal in their support. Mr. Linfield became the chairman of the newly-formed League of Helpers of Gifford House as well as being a governor. One of their achievements was to organise an entertainment every Wednesday evening. It was they who had arranged for the Christmas Sale to be held in the gas showrooms, which, in 1944, for example, raised £288. We shall be seeing their influence from time to time, though much was handled behind the scenes. Sadly, but inevitably, the hospital lost some of its Governors who had given it some excellent service. On 16 June 1943 Sir William Goschen died, having been chairman of the Finance Committee for 24 years. His wise and sound judgment, his devotion and zeal had been very highly appreciated. A memorial service was held at St Michael's, Cornhill on 22 June, attended by many representatives of the City of London and the financial institutions with which Sir William was connected; Mr. Hay represented Gifford House. A second memorial service, held at the London Hospital Church, on the following day, was conducted by the Bishop of Stepney. Queen Mary was represented by Major John Wickham and Lady Juliet Duff represented Gifford House. She wrote this tribute to him:

> For 26 years he had been a faithful friend and wise counsellor. Although, with his other work for the Joint Council of the Red Cross and St John and his Chairmanship of the London Hospital, he seemed to have more to do than was humanly possible, when he attended our Committee meetings he always made us feel that Gifford House and its well-being was his first and only thought. We can never be sufficiently grateful to him for all that he did for us, and we shall not easily forget him.

Mr. Algernon Hay died on 1 February 1945. Lady Juliet, speaking of his loss, paid tribute to his companionship and his splendid work for Gifford House. Miss Fletcher described his loss as that of

> a loyal and faithful friend, whose affectionate and personal interest we had known since the early days of Gifford House, Roehampton, in 1919.
>
> Being disabled himself and unable to walk without the aid of two sticks, Mr. Hay had a sympathetic understanding of the patients' point of view. He was especially interested in the recreations for the men: games tournaments, whist drives and entertainments during the winter months, and the garden for their outdoor pleasure. He spent much time and thought in keeping the garden gay with colour all the year round, for the enjoyment of the men who cannot easily get beyond the garden. His kindly cheerfulness and friendly talks with the bed patients were always greatly appreciated by them.
>
> Many subscribers will have received his personal acknowledgment for, during his office as Vice-Chairman, Mr. Hay endeavoured to acknowledge almost every subscription himself and to add some little note of interest to the sender.

Perhaps the most sincere tribute to Mr. Hay is expressed in the words of a patient—'He knew the name of every leaf in the garden, and loved every bit of Gifford House. In the six years I have been here I have never seen him pass by anyone without a cheery word, or a joke. He was one of the kindest men I have ever known'.

The third loss was that of Sir Lisle Webb, who died on 7 October 1945; he had served the hospital since its opening in 1919 and had resigned as Chairman of the Governors for health reasons in October 1943, but had consented to be a Patron of the Home.

Another Patron who died, in 1945, was Mr. J.D. Charrington, OBE, who had lent his home and grounds to the Home from May 1919 to August, 1933. And in the same month, December, Sir Farquhar Buzzard, Bart., KCVO, FRCP, the honorary consulting physician, also died, having contributed his skill and knowledge for the patients under his care.

But whilst the years took their (inevitable) toll and as Father Time continued on his inexorable way, one can see that Gifford House had matured as an institution, thanks not least to the distinguished service by people with exceptional gifts. It was a maturity that at no time showed any tendency to ossify or to be complacent, but rather to be witness to the vision of its Founder, as it faced the challenges of the second half of the century.

55 *Bill Impey (second from right), with friends and escorts on the promenade by Heene Terrace*

CHAPTER 11

◆

MATURITY

One of the most remarkable aspects of Gifford House is the way in which its finances have prospered during the last 50 years. Having said that, the story of how the finances were nurtured is one of sheer hard graft by the administrative and financial staff, together with dedicated hard work by many volunteers.

To give some idea of the scope of the task, the income for the Home in 1946 was £13,842; the expenses totalled £20,730. In 1996 the figures were £1,029,181 and £1,505,336 respectively. In most years Gifford House has operated with a deficit. This is not unexpected because, as we have seen in earlier chapters, official funding, not in itself ungenerous, worked in favour of the 'average' patient. As the Minister of Pensions said at the opening ceremony in 1919, there would always be a need to make up the difference between official funding and the actual needs of the patients.

The sources of voluntary finance have been threefold: pure fund-raising by local effort, contributions received from military and other charitable bodies and appeals to the public, often on a national scale.

One of the key aspects of local fund-raising after the Second World War was the work of what was known as the Appeals Committee. Their scope was unlimited. They would investigate any method which might have a financial benefit. This could be the pursuit of projects involving the collection of soap and packet labels (to claim cash from the promoter), keys and metal objects for trading in, and arranging special events. In April 1955 the Spirella Fashion Foundation firm presented a display in the Pier Pavilion, strictly ladies only (even the manager locked himself in his office), and over £60 was raised for Gifford House. A model railway exhibition held in October 1960 was attended by 12,696 people and raised £217 4s. 9d. The Committee had considered staging a boxing display but the expected return on the outlay was judged not to justify the effort. On 7 March 1967, one of the matches in the World Open Snooker Championship was staged at Gifford House: Rex Williams beat Joe Davis by three frames to two and, after the contest, the players treated the audience to a display of stunning trick shots. Wilf Page, the landlord of *The Cricketers* in Broadwater, set up a bar in the Quiet Room(!) and donated his profit to the Home. Altogether, the evening raised £189.

The Committee would make appeals for home-made marmalade which could be sold for the Home and the press cuttings from the post-war years describe many events which caught the imagination locally. In 1956, the Appeals Committee agreed that it had had 'a successful year's "begging" '. That was basically the nature of its task and many people were to become involved in its activities. It is an involvement which had remained steady ever since the arrival in Worthing. A young lady named Shirley Woodward sold raffle tickets for the Christmas Fund in 1943 and 1945. Shirley still has the receipts signed by A.G. Linfield and Miss Fletcher; her future husband, Matt Sullivan, was to find a niche in Gifford House 50 years later where he could receive the full care he needed.

We have seen how major charitable institutions provided invaluable financial support at critical times. This continued in the post-war years, and was later to figure prominently in the financing of

56   *Lt. Gen Sir Brian Horrocks with the BBC Film Unit recording his appeal*

large-scale building projects (as we shall see). Prominent among these charities have been the Army Benevolent Fund, the Royal Air Force Benevolent Fund, King George's Fund for Sailors and regimental associations which retain a continuing interest through frequent contributions. Significantly, their interest is in members of their associations who come within the ambit of the care available at Gifford House. Thus the very principles which motivated Lady Ripon are still being followed.

The third major area of financial support came through appeals on a nationwide basis. Advertisements were placed in national newspapers and publications, as they still are. But the area where the greatest benefit was felt was in the appeals put out on radio and television. On the former, appeals were made by Group Captain Bader (twice), Mr. Cuthbert Fitzherbert, Major Sir Brunel Cohen, Sir Compton Mackenzie, Dame Vera Lynn and Kenneth More. These appeals would raise around £5,000 each. The cash raised from these appeals was used to meet the deficits that were inevitably incurred. The donations were a great fillip to the Appeals committee and all who had the interest of Gifford House at heart. But the real benefits were intangible at the time, in that a massive amount of good will was created and Gifford House was regularly in the public eye. The full measure of this will never be known but the impact is still being felt in the level of legacies which are received. These legacies have made all the difference between survival and despair, as demonstrated by the summary of the financial situation (see p.115).

Not surprisingly, the most successful appeal was on television. The presenter was Lt. Gen. Sir Brian Horrocks, who had served with the Middlesex Regiment in 1914, had been wounded in Russia in 1919 and awarded the MC. In the Second World War he was awarded the DSO, and was GOC of the British Army of the Rhine before retiring in 1949. From then to 1963 he was the

Gentleman Usher, Black Rod, in the House of Lords. His appeal in 1963 raised the splendid sum of £14,063. When Sir Brian first visited Gifford House he was well-known to the patients through his television series *Into Battle* which gave graphic descriptions of significant engagements during the war. There is no doubt that his eyes were opened by the cheerfulness of the patients and by the facilities which were available. In his appeal he said:

> I think this is one of the happiest places I have ever been in—but you know that sort of cheerfulness needs great courage. And I always leave here a humble man.

He became a great friend to the Home, and a patient wrote:

> To those of us who have been privileged to meet him and to enjoy his conversation, his characteristic poise is of even more marked distinction and quality, and one is deeply impressed by his friendliness, understanding and the magnetism of his personality.

The organisation behind this appeal bears relating. Altogether, 69 helpers were involved and 49,879 leaflets distributed, 50 national and provincial newspapers circulated and about 1,400 letters sent to individuals who might be interested. The first donation was received by hand 25 minutes after the broadcast. Eventually, 7,602 letters were received, each was acknowledged. This is a pertinent reminder of the role of administrative back-up to any such appeal, and those who took part helped in sowing the seed which still bears a harvest in the interest shown by friends and benefactors today.

What was the outcome of this concentration on finance? Probably one which would be the envy of many a charity but, if so, then a reflection of the good stewardship of the officers and administrators. The improvement over the decades is shown thus:

	Cumulative Value of Legacies	Cumulative Value of Deficits
1960	£68,864	£85,217
1965	£129,957	£60,723
1970	£205,056	£64,019
1975	£283,687	£130,893
1980	£755,999	£(129,454)
1985	£962,581	£(305,734)
1990	£2,022,169	£(40,496)
1995	£2,141,690	£646,724

Apart from 11 years beginning in the mid-70s, Gifford House has always operated on an annual deficit. Legacies have enabled the annual deficits to be absorbed, and the surplus invested for income. Without this very practical support, the closure of this wonderful institution would have been a distinct possibility.

In 1965, Bernard, 16th Duke of Norfolk became Joint Honorary Treasurer with the 9th Duke of Richmond and Gordon. The Duke and his wife, Lavinia, and members of their family, always paid a visit to Gifford House on Christmas Day and, after his death, his family continued his interest in Gifford House and their Christmas visits. The Duchess Lavinia had become Vice-President in 1980 and after her death, her daughter, Lady Sarah Clutton, succeeded her in this role in 1996.

One of the dominant features of Gifford House has been the atmosphere which has prevailed. There have been exceptional people, it is true, but everyone who stops to look back paints a picture of cheerfulness. One such person is Miss Daphne Morris who became Matron in 1965 after 17 years in Princess Mary's Royal Air Force Nursing Service with special experience as Sister in Charge of a Burns Unit. She was familiar with patients needing long-term care but she herself

57 *Ron Fisher (left) and Leslie Longman (right), with Carl Grosvenor*

was the first to receive care, for her mother died shortly after her appointment and Miss Morris recalls the warmth of sympathy she felt from the patients at the time: 'I had come to help them but they did so much more for me … I realised how fortunate I was to have the opportunity to have such close contact with the patients'.

She recalls how the little things were often the most appreciated. 'I remember suggesting to a patient with no hands that if we put Velcro on his trousers he could manage this with his stumps and become independent. He said this transformed his life!' And staff continued to be amazed at what a disabled man could do to live as normal a life as possible. Sir Brian Horrocks mentioned Dick Taylor, who had been hit in the head by a shell splinter in 1915. 'From that moment, normal life as we know it, ceased for him altogether.' His wife died and his disability got worse but for 10 years he had been cared for in Gifford House and, although he had only one hand, amazed everyone by being able to peel an orange all in one piece.

Sometimes the patients' friends would help. Such was the case with George White, disabled in the Great War. He was so helpless that he could not even turn over the page of a book without help but two of his friends pulled pocket-sized books to pieces and joined the pages into continuous strips. These were fed on to rollers driven by a gramophone motor controlled by a piece of string. By pulling on the string with his teeth, George was able to turn the pages. The local Guides and Scouts were enlisted to help with gumming together more books.

Not that all patients conformed, and Matrons faced constant battles over trifling and not-so-trifling matters. For example, Ron Fisher tended to be something of a rebel. When he died in 1996, stories of his escapades and confrontations with 'authority' still abounded; perhaps it was his training as a football referee! His driving style was legendary or, rather, his sheer exuberance when behind the wheel; roundabouts were often taken in a anti-clockwise direction—yet never an accident. And somehow the nursing staff kept cool when he forcefully expressed his views on matters of treatment or administration. Two of Ron's compatriots, 'Nick' Nicholls and Leslie Longman, are still in Gifford House. While Nick is still working on his paintings, Leslie, who has been a patient since 1962, has always been active and heavily involved in the life of the Home. Although his participation in photography, wine-making, sewing and caravanning has reduced, he still drives a specially-adapted Citroen, although he has no hands or legs. Such characters make Gifford House a place which is always lively and vibrant.

Miss Morris had the idea of finding a mascot for the Home and 28 patients boarded their coach in October 1969 to visit a breeder of Pyrenean Mountain dogs in the New Forest. An 11-month-old bitch, Penny, was selected from eight puppies and brought to Gifford House where a patient, Tommy Mansford, was appointed her handler and groom. She turned out to be too boisterous and had to be returned. Her successor, Juno, was older and more sedate, weighing 122lbs and standing 52 inches on her hind legs. Tommy claimed that she was lazy and preferred sleeping all day but they both became popular characters in the streets of Worthing, until Juno died in November 1974.

Although pets have not played a prominent part in the Worthing Home they have had 'their exits and their entrances'. In the summer of 1957, a tame jackdaw was caught by three men and two small boys in the Goring Road after a ¾-hour chase. They took the bird to Gifford House where it was put in the charge of Bill Middleton, a nature lover. While a cage was being made for the bird, it escaped. Not so in the case of a mynah bird given to the home; it developed a wonderful imitation of the distinctive laugh of the member of the domestic staff who looked after her. The bird gave great pleasure to the patients. One of them taught this bird to wolf-whistle, somewhat to the embarrassment of a group of visiting nuns. The bird was confined to non-public quarters!

Our history has mentioned many times, since the early days in Roehampton, Miss Beth Fletcher. She had been appointed Matron in 1921 and finally retired from Gifford House on 13 June 1959. At the time, this was the longest period of service of any member of staff and she had been one of the most popular. A particularly fine expression of the respect and love in which she was held is shown in an illuminated address which the patients presented to her on 6 January 1959, clearly hoping it would persuade her not to retire:

58 *Tommy Mansford with Juno*

It is with great pleasure that we take this opportunity of expressing the gratitude we owe you and to record our debt in this dedication of the care you show us every day.

For many years you have been Matron of Gifford House, an indulgent and understanding Mother to whom we have brought our plaints and our whimpers, our problems and suggestions. Never once have you failed us during these years.

With your guidance Gifford House became a home and a sanctuary for the wounded and disabled men to whom you have been a special providence. Your ministrations have been far from easy, the work upon which you have been engaged and so worthily carried out has been a token of love.

The patients are conscious of this and acknowledge it with thankfulness, through your human feeling our lives have been brightened and our infirmities alleviated. Gentle in manner, resolute in execution you have tackled duty and problems with equal ease, ever ready to put wrongs right, overlooking faults you have stressed the virtues. Your patient devotion and compassionate interest have inspired us all, and your loyalty has made us not forgotten men but partakers of a new life where hope and happiness are ever present.

That you may long be with us is the affectionate hope of your children The Patients of Gifford House.

There is a touching sequel to her story. Although she might have thought that she had left Gifford House behind her when she retired, she did in fact return when she became in need of nursing care, and spent the last 18 months of her life in Gifford House, in her old rooms. She died on 9 December 1975.

Ten years earlier, a link with the past had been broken when Lady Juliet Duff, Lady Ripon's daughter, died on 27 September 1965 aged 84. Lady Juliet had worked with great vigour after her mother's death to ensure that funds were raised so that a perpetual memorial to Lady Ripon could be realised. Her efforts led to the ability to fund The Queen Alexandra Home, as we have seen. She had been Vice-President of Gifford House since 1919 and her interest had never waned. She lived a very full and active life; among her friends were Somerset Maugham, Hilaire Belloc, Stravinsky, Picasso, General de Gaulle and Sir Winston Churchill, and she was a frequent guest at Downing Street. She had a deeply personal interest in the patients and staff who remembered her for her many kindnesses. She was their enthusiastic and affectionate friend. The family link was continued when her son, Sir Michael Duff, became Vice-President in succession to his mother. With his own charismatic gifts and sense of humour and fun, he became a most popular visitor to Gifford House from his home in Wales. After his death in 1980, when Lavinia, Duchess of Norfolk succeeded him, the support of the Norfolk family was underlined.

A sense of humour has always pervaded the home. Dick Rolyat, a patient, wrote in 1969 of the kinds of comments made to him as he sat on the promenade in his wheelchair. When one person asked him where he was wounded, he replied 'Armentiers, 14 November 1915' only to be told that there was no engagement at that time! Kindly ladies would ask him how he got his accident; when he replied that it was no accident but 'by malicious intent of those horrid Germans' they would immediately tell him their family histories. One lady asked him why he did not have a motorised chair. He told her that as he had fits of unconsciousness, it was not possible. 'What does it feel like to be unconscious?', she asked. And, leaning over the side of his chair one day, examining the tyre, a kind lady asked if he had dropped something; our bald friend replied: 'Yes, my hair net' and got a 'wigging' from her for being frivolous. Now these are good tales—and a fine example of Gifford House humour, for they were all the product of the fertile imagination of Dick Taylor— or Rolyat!

Some patients had a splendid war record. One such was Joseph Davies who came to Gifford House in October 1972 as a holiday patient. When the 1914 war broke out he was in the hills in India, having previously served in Khartoum, Egypt and Gibraltar. He won the VC at Delville Wood on the Somme. He was also the proud possessor of the Russian Gold Cross (equivalent, he said, to the VC). During the fighting, he had been hit in the shoulder but fought on for 4½ hours and took the position. Then he handed over the trench to a corporal and struggled back 40 yards to the Allied lines. He rolled into the trench and saw two men in blue uniforms whom he took for officers of some of the allied forces. They took his name and number. Mr. Davies was at the time the only one to hold the two decorations. He returned for another holiday in 1974 and became a permanent patient in 1975, and died on 6 December in that same year.

In November 1953 the *Worthing Herald* featured the situation of 23-year old Nigel Harvey who came to Gifford House as a holiday patient. Nigel had entered the Army when he was 17 and had contracted infantile paralysis when serving with the Royal Corps of Signals in Malaya. He completely lost the use of his arms, but had fairly good movement in his feet and legs. When he was in a military hospital near Oxford, his physiotherapist remembered a piece of apparatus she had seen in her native New Zealand. It consisted of hollow metal cylinders clipped to the leg just above the knee and connected to a footplate which rocked in any direction when activated by the foot. The movement was carried upwards on metal arms which Nigel was able to use for typing letters, albeit slowly. He said: 'The great thing is that I can deal with my own correspondence. I can fold a letter, place it in the envelope, seal and stamp it'. He could also turn over the leaves of a book, and a knife, fork or spoon could be attached to the device. Nigel has lead a fully active life for many years and has kept in touch, returning for the occasional visit. His mechanical 'apparatus' now extends to a specially adapted car which, still with no use of his arms, he can drive by means

59 *The kitchen before renovation in 1967*

of a foot-controlled metal plate on the floor of the car. He passed his driving test first time after 15 hours at the 'wheel'.

After the war, it was necessary for the Governors to look to the adequacy of the accommodation but their deliberations were restricted by the lack of funds to do any significant planning. Their idea of establishing a building fund is recorded as far back as 1945, the need for an additional ward being identified as the top priority. Work began on the ward in 1946 and it was opened by the Duchess of Gloucester on 17 October 1947. The ward was named after Mrs. Verena Hay and, thanks to a very generous response to an appeal, it was completed without incurring any debt. This meant that there were now four large and two small wards. During Her Royal Highness' tour, the new Quiet Room was used for the first time. The next significant project was the plan to have an 'Occupational Therapeutic Room' and an invalid chair store. The new Department was opened at the end of 1952 and proved to be a great benefit to patients interested in handicrafts. In 1959 a new physiotherapy department was completed; benefiting from a very generous donation, it was fitted out with the most up-to-date equipment. Its popularity and value is shown by the fact that in the following year just under 4,000 treatments were carried out.

Anyone who has a particular interest in what might be termed the 'archaeology of buildings' would find Gifford House to be full of new discoveries, from the initial 'R' of the Ralli family on the weathervane to the pomegranates on the ceiling decorations in the original house. Over the last 30 years or so, that has remained largely unaltered but the buildings which have been grafted on to it have undergone significant changes in order to provide appropriate medical care. In 1967 the wards were upgraded by the provision of suspended ceilings to hide the roof trusses, separate lighting for each bedspace and thermostatically controlled heating. The central kitchen was extensively modernised as were the central lavatory facilities and bathrooms. The old iron baths, four in line, separated only by curtains had served their life-span! New oil-fired central heating was installed. The builders were in for nearly eight months. This work was made possible by an anonymous donation and legacies.

In 1970 a Sun Lounge was built in memory of Mrs. Gwendoline Linfield, the wife of the Chairman, A.G. Linfield, who had herself been a governor of Gifford House. Built across the north end of the Home, close to the chapel, it is one of the favourite places for sitting in a sunny aspect and for viewing the frequent arrivals and departures of vehicles and people.

Four years later, the entrance to the Home was extensively improved by installing a large canopy over the entrance with automatic glass sliding doors. New large picture windows were installed in the Day Room. In that same year, 'The Elms' was demolished. It had been used as staff accommodation but there was a distinct change in needs as staff gradually preferred to live at home. It was unproductive to have this building largely lying idle but in order to give some accommodation, a bungalow was built in its place thanks to the Royal Air Force Benevolent Fund, the Dulverton Trust and the Hayward Foundation, and this served to house some senior nursing staff for a few years. It is now occupied by the gardener and his family.

In 1975, the family of Sir Arthur Linfield, who had died the previous year, gave a unique collection of some 500 orchids and an Orchid House. A plaque inside reads: 'It was always the wish of one who loved his flowers that others should enjoy them also—therefore this Orchid House is given by members of his family in affectionate remembrance'. In the same year the new Occupational Therapy Department was built and equipped, thanks to the Army Benevolent Fund.

Beginning in October 1980 the first phase of building a new central dining room and the enlargement and modernisation of the bathroom complex was started. Previously, meals had been served on the wards and in the Day Room. A number of alterations had to be carried out to achieve these improvements—and that is another mark of the way in which alterations have been made: one idea, once conceived, impacts other areas and the need for a detailed, integrated plan becomes essential. The 'new look', which the completion of the project produced, is now accepted as part of the building but, when opened, brought new colour and light to the main corridors and circulation areas. In 1985, a new Physiotherapy Department was created through the generosity of the Sir Jules Thorn Charitable Trust.

But perhaps the most traumatic, certainly the most far-reaching, development came in 1987 with the plan to replace the wards which had been in service since 1933 and one which had been opened in 1947 (and took more demolition). The wards were of the open-bedded 'Nightingale' design. Although modernised in 1967, structural problems were appearing; there was also severe heat loss as the walls were single-skin brick. Studies of other Homes were made, and then the thoughts of the Gifford House team were put on paper and discussed with the Technical Services Department of the builders James Longley & Co. Ltd. of Crawley. The plans were therefore based on experience in running the Home and knowing the needs of the patients and staff. The old wards would be replaced by two new wings providing accommodation in one-, two-, three-and four- bed units. The builders came on site on 7 September, 1987 and in October had to contend with a rainfall of 9ins. in three weeks! Photographs of the project show how detailed the planning had to be. The first wing replaced two of the old wards and, such was the difference in concept, that some people found it difficult to see how the new buildings would be an improvement! But such is the impression given at any building site and as soon as the fitting up began and the beauty of the American Ash woodwork apparent, then a proper appreciation was possible. The first wing was completed on 3 June 1988 and named 'Elizabeth' after the President, Queen Elizabeth the Queen

Mother. The second wing, opened the next year, was named 'Lavinia' after the Vice-President, Lavinia, Duchess of Norfolk. The project had meant a tremendous upheaval in the life of the Home. No Open Days were held in those two years, fewer holiday patients were able to come and beds which became vacant were not immediately filled. On one occasion the main telephone cable was cut—but such are the hazards of a major project conducted on a restricted site which has to remain operational. The results are the striking buildings which grace Gifford House today, and it is amazing how visitors comment on the airy aspect of the wards, the beauty of the wood. The wards are almost completely hidden from the road, so visitors at Open Day have their eyes opened as they tour the building for the first time.

Another major project was completed by the installation of a hydrotherapy pool in the area occupied by the old coach-house. It was opened on 23 March 1992 and was achieved through a special appeal. It is fair to say that this is one of the most popular treatment facilities for the patients, and not least by those who come on holiday breaks and who are unable to enjoy such facilities through their local health authorities.

The summary of all this activity is that Gifford House is able to offer facilities for the care of patients which are not only up-to-date but, arguably, in advance of those available in many institutions. One would imagine that Lady Ripon and Mrs. Hay would have thoroughly approved of these changes, which were brought about by the far-sighted planning by the Governors, the most generous response of donors and fund-raisers, and the dedication of all the staff.

Far-sighted planning does not, however, happen by accident. The significant changes above were the direct result of conscious thought and action. As such, one has to look for the source of this activity, and the guiding light behind the Home. From 1945 to 1974, this was the role of its Chairman, Arthur Linfield, who had welcomed Mrs. Hay and her 'Boys' to Worthing in 1933 in his capacity as Chairman of Worthing Rotary Club. Mr. Linfield, or 'A.G.' as he was affectionately known, brought to Gifford House considerable qualities which were to prove invaluable in its development. Initially, he introduced Gifford House to Worthing through his contacts with local people, especially those who were in positions of influence in the community. In many ways, he was responsible for integrating Gifford House into Worthing. Not least valuable were his interests in the Hospital world. He was Chairman of Worthing Hospital, and also of the SW Metropolitan Region Hospital Board. Interestingly, one of the issues he had to face was whether or not Gifford House should become part of the new National Health Service. Here was someone who could see the advantages and disadvantages. Reading the minutes of the Governors' meetings, it is clear that they were firmly in favour of retaining their independence. Mr. Linfield appears to have given them full scope for airing the pros and cons; once the decision was made to remain independent, then he was the firm advocate of that decision. The Annual Reports of the post-war years mention frequently the appropriateness of that decision, which time has justified. His invitations for the patients to visit his nurseries at Thakeham for strawberry teas in the summer were always popular. One of his daughters, Mollie, recalls that Gifford House 'was his first love. He loved people and he had great affection for the men. He enjoyed going there, it meant so much to him'. At that time he had no idea that Mollie would one day experience his affection for Gifford House but, after teaching painting to many of the men for 13 years, she too was able to understand the honour in helping. Reading the minutes, one gets the impression that 'A.G.' was someone who went calmly about his business, with acute and shrewd judgment, almost unflappable, bringing people together in decision-making and, once having agreed a course of action, doing all that was necessary to implement it. His own contacts were invaluable in this respect and Gifford House has been the beneficiary of much practical support thanks to his influence and persuasion. He was a bridge-builder, and a man of compassion, thoughtful and kind. His physical presence was powerful yet he was not one to assert himself; in fact, he had a distinct preference for doing things quietly, not letting one hand

60 *The Duke and Duchess of Norfolk during a Christmas visit*

know what the other was doing. He received public recognition for his services; he was made a Commander of the Order of the British Empire and a Knight Commander of the Royal Victorian Order, though sadly he died in April, before the knighting ceremony.

At his Memorial Service, the Rt. Revd. Simon Phipps, the first Bishop of Horsham, spoke of him with great affection although he had known him for only 18 months. He recalled visiting Sir Arthur when he was dying. He was calm, and quiet and remembered that the bishop had only recently married; he asked the bishop to choose an orchid for his wife and, when he left Sir Arthur, the bishop found that the message had been conveyed to Sir Arthur's staff and he was conducted to the orchid house. To many who knew him, this will be a typical action of a thoughtful, modest and considerate man; much of the well-being of Gifford House today is due to those very qualities.

His successor was Major-General Sir James Bowes-Lyon who was to continue the work put in hand by his predecessor whom he had known since becoming a governor himself. Sir James, with his military background, strengthened the links with the Services which are so important not only to Gifford House but also that ex-servicemen may know of the facilities and care which are available to them. He showed a distinct interest in the facilities for the patients; this showed in the practical matters of buildings and on the social side. As a steward of the Brighton Races, he introduced outings to the races which were to prove extremely popular (if not monetarily rewarding to the punters!). He was also instrumental in enabling patients to attend the Queen's Birthday Parade (Trooping the Colour) which remains one of the highlights of the year and is particularly enjoyed by ex-Guardsmen who have previously taken part in it themselves.

Sir James was still in office planning the new Occupational Therapy Department, a project dear to his heart, when his death on 18 December 1977 brought a deep sense of loss to the Home, for much had been achieved under his guidance and leadership.

His successor, Major-General Sir Philip Ward, is still in post. The advances and improvements during his 20 years as Chairman, not least in the gardens, have been largely brought about by his enthusiasm and energy. His contacts, with the patients individually and in so many fields together with his appointment as Lord Lieutenant of West Sussex, have meant that the needs of Gifford House and what it has to offer have been brought before a wide range of people and institutions. He has continued the tradition of forward-thinking and innovation which has always been the mark of Gifford House. The re-building projects described above, costing over £2 million, would have been unimaginable to his predecessors yet, significantly enough, a sign that the remarks made by the Marquis of Ripon in 1919 are still true, namely that the ripples of the work begun by his wife are still being felt in a very different age.

Those differences are not only social but are reflected in legislation which has altered the course of Gifford House. This was most noticeable in the passing of the Community Care Act which came into force in 1993. This Act radically re-structured the financing of the sick, disabled and elderly, transferring funding from a national to a local level. Local teams would henceforward assess the needs of an individual patient, decide the care they thought appropriate and which was within their budget. To a Home admitting patients from all over the British Isles, this caused a significant increase in workload, the sheer number of local authorities to be contacted together with the weighty contracts which have to be completed (for one county this is 1in. thick). The threat was real enough. In September 1982 23 patients were war pensioners and funded as such but by 1992 this number had reduced to seven. Until 1985, eight beds had been funded by the Area Health Authority (one of the achievements of Sir Arthur Linfield); this erosion of reliable funding brought about feelings of uncertainty, which Mrs. Hay and her team would have understood. There was also a threat in this to the holiday scheme, for local Social Service departments would be far tougher on their decisions. Additionally, the Registered Homes Act, 1994 brought in more control over how such an establishment is run. All this has not stopped the current Matron, Mrs. Mary Childs, from ensuring that the nursing care, given in a supportive environment, is still the distinctive characteristic of Gifford House.

The impact has been that the Governors have had to strive hard to maintain the unique identity of Gifford House. There has been a continuing provision of short-term bed occupancy. Patients tend to be older and in need of a great deal of care, with further pressure on the nursing staff. Consequently, more people each year are receiving care; ex-services associations are often in touch about their members' needs. There is some financial shortfall as a result, which makes it all the more necessary to exercise prudent stewardship of the funds which have been built up over the years.

Relationships with the local community have been important ever since Mrs. Hay began to make known the aims of Gifford House to the residents of Worthing. In those early days, one of the popular ways of fund-raising was to hold Flag Days, involving a mountain of administration and organisation. In 1964 this practice was discontinued and the Secretary, Miss J.M. Holgate, introduced the concept of the Open Day. These days have enabled local people to discover what really goes on 'the other side of the wall', as is often quipped. The second Saturday in July is part of the local calendar, and the house and grounds are always full of friends and supporters. Key to the success of this event has been the wonderful support received from public figures who readily agree to open the proceedings. The most frequent supporter has been Dame Vera Lynn who has appeared six times, as well as paying other informal visits. The military bands have been superb in their attendance.

61 *Welcoming Queen Elizabeth The Queen Mother are, from left: The 9th Duke of Richmond and Gordon, Sir Michael Duff, Mr. A.G. Linfield and the 16th Duke of Norfolk.*

The patronage of members of the Royal Family has been a great strength to patients and staff. Since the early 1950s, visits have been made by Princess Mary, The Princess Royal, Princess Alexandra and Prince Philip but the most frequent visitor has been Queen Elizabeth, the Queen Mother, who became President of Gifford House in 1953. She had visited Gifford House three times before the war when she was Duchess of York, and her visits in 1966, 1979, 1983, 1989 and 1992 have been most popular. It is intriguing to read the notes which set out the actions required in planning for such visits. For her visit in April 1992 there were nine weeks to make the preparations. Discussions with the staff of Clarence House were followed by detailed planning with the police who, early on the day, made a thorough search of the whole building. One unexpected result for one of the patients was that his First World War revolver, which he had kept as a souvenir, had to be confiscated under the necessarily strict security rules. Links were established with the Central Office of Information and the Queen's personal bodyguard, and Miss Holgate and the Matron, Mrs. Mary Childs, walked the route over 20 times. The patients found the preparations a fascinating phenomenon to watch, and the whole staff put on a splendid team effort to make the day a great success. The weather was atrocious but umbrellas had been ordered; in spite of promises, they had not arrived by 11am and it was discovered that they were going around Worthing in a Post Office delivery van—and the Post Office knew there were no deliveries allowed that day! With police intervention, the van arrived in the nick of time.

One of those endearing traditions which could never be planned started during the visit of The Queen Mother to Gifford House in 1966. One of the feathers on her hat fluttered to the ground, and she readily agreed that it should be retained as a souvenir of her visit. When she visited in 1976 and saw it framed in a photograph, she gave another feather which had fallen out in the car. On her visit in 1979 she invited Miss Holgate to cut another feather from her hat. The Press photographers, who were not party to the understanding, thought this was an attempt by Miss Holgate to 'snaffle' a feather for her own purposes, and she received unexpected press coverage and had to explain that the event was all above board!

When The Queen Mother celebrated her 90th birthday, Gifford House was represented at the Birthday Tribute held in Horse Guards Parade on 27 June 1990. The party of 13, patients and staff members, depicted the change in wheelchairs and uniforms over the years, starting with a wicker spinal carriage through to the most modern electric chair. Military and staff uniforms matched the period of the chairs. The party set out at 7am. The rehearsals under military direction were less daunting than feared. The heat was palpable, the arrangements for drinking and feeding worked satisfactorily and eventually the great moment came for them to take their place, 28D in the great procession. This was at 6.40pm. A coachload of patients and staff were in the stands to watch the performance. The Parade was seen nationally on television and was a moving occasion. 16 hours after leaving Worthing a tired, limp but elated team returned to Gifford House.

62 *Sir James Bowes-Lyon with The Queen Mother during her visit in 1976*

63   *A welcome for Her Majesty from (left to right): Mr. F. Burge, Accountant, Miss J.M. Holgate, Chief Executive, Mrs. M. Childs, Matron, Dr. J. Dand, Medical Officer, Mr. R. Parsons, Vice-Chairman and Sir Philip Ward, Chairman, 1992*

Tales could be told of many other aspects of Gifford House, of romances and weddings, of patients who have, by their courage and cheerfulness, made a lasting mark in the memories of staff and patients alike, of benefactors and supporters who have given of their time, money and skills. Characters among the staff are recalled with affection and humour. To describe these fully would require a volume which is outside the scope of this history—perhaps one day it will be written. But our questions as we look back over the history of this institution are: was Lady Ripon's vision fulfilled? and was Mrs. Hay's faith justified?

The affirmative answer lies in the very building and people who are Gifford House. Whatever future changes may be faced, there is within it a legacy of love and care, and a tradition of cheerfulness and courage. As the years pass, the number of those who remember the past days will inevitably diminish. Hopefully this history will help to keep alive not only their memory but an awareness of the unique quality of care which has always been its mark.

The postscript to this should be with the person who has served Gifford House for the longest period of time of anyone in its history, Miss J.M. Holgate, MVO who, as Secretary and then as Chief Executive, had the responsibility for the oversight of its many plans and activities. Immersed in its ethos for 46 years, hers was the inspiration for this book; it is proper that she should contribute her own special perceptions to conclude this history:

> I joined the staff at Gifford House in May, 1951. I was just 19. From the moment I arrived I was aware that I was entering a very special place and that I was among very special people.

As I prepared for my retirement, I realised that I was the end of a line. I was the last one who had had the good fortune to work with those who had witnessed the conception of the vision which founded the Queen Alexandra Hospital Home at Gifford House nearly 80 years ago. Those who had faithfully pursued its ideals inspiring one and then another to join them. I thought of the patients and the tales they had had to tell me over the years. I had seen nearly 500 names added to the Book of Remembrance.

The story lay around me. Photographs, files of correspondence, press cuttings, house magazines, minutes of meetings and in my memory, too. I had a great desire to share the story. I asked David Farrant for his help. He began to read, to research and to ask questions. He soon became fascinated by what he found and set to work. I am so grateful to him for the meticulous way in which he has sifted through the archives and listened to my recollections and reminiscences. I know that those whose story he has told would be grateful, too. I know because I have shared my life with many of them. They were my friends.

The need today may seem to be far removed from that which inspired Lady Ripon's vision but Gifford House has a tradition of adapting to meet the needs of the day. May it long continue to do so.

APPENDIX

◆

Chairmen

1919-1920. . . . . Colonel E.F. Badeley CBE
1920-1940. . . . . Mrs Verena Hay CBE
1940-1943. . . . . Colonel Sir A. Lisle Webb KBE CB CMG
1943-1945. . . . . Major-General Sir John Kennedy KBE CB CMG DSO
1945-1974. . . . . Sir Arthur Linfield KCVO CBE JP
1974-1977. . . . . Major-General Sir James Bowes-Lyon KCVO CB OBE DSO
1978- . . . . Major-General Sir Philip Ward KCVO CBE

Matrons

1919. . . . . Miss L. Pollock
1920. . . . . Miss M. Harte
1921-1959. . . . . Miss L. Fletcher
1959. . . . . Miss P. Dewey
1960-1965. . . . . Miss A. Hampton
1966. . . . . Miss D. Hawker
1967-1978. . . . . Miss D. Morris
1978-1985. . . . . Mrs A. Warner
1985- . . . . Mrs M. Childs

Medical Officers

1919. . . . . Dr. J. Todesco
1919-1959. . . . . Dr. O. Gotch
1959-1962. . . . . Dr. R. Stevens
1962. . . . . Dr. J. Walsh
1963-1978. . . . . Dr. P. Murphy
1978. . . . . Dr. K. Rooke
1978-1984. . . . . Dr. B. Cormick
1984-1989. . . . . Dr. J. Ferries
1989- . . . . Dr. J. Dand

INDEX

◆